RANDOM
THOUGHTS

RANDOM THOUGHTS

Vandana Sinha

PARTRIDGE
A Penguin Random House Company

To order additional copies of this book, contact
Partridge India
000 800 10062 62
orders.india@partridgepublishing.com

www.partridgepublishing.com/india

CONTENTS

Acknowledgements 13

Dedication 15

Author's Note 17

1: ME***IN THE WOODS 19

2: ME***WHERE HAS IT GONE? 20

3: ME***INTO THE MISTY HAZE 21

4: ME***I SAW LIFE AT THE 'GATES OF DEATH' 22

5: ME***"WHO SAID THIS?" 23

6: ME***PAPER BALLS..24

7: ME***THE WILD BERRY 25

8: ME***ALWAYS BY MY SIDE 27

9: ME***THE SUNNY DREAMS 28

10: ME***TO BE CONVINCED...29

11: ME***SING-SONG MEMORIES 31

12: ME***GAY ABUNDANCE 33

13: ASPECT of LIFE***PAST 34

14: ME***RAVISHING TRESSES...36

15: ASPECT of LIFE***HAPPINESS AND POSITIVITY.......................38

16: ASPECT of LIFE***"WHOEVER GOES UP . ." 40

17: ASPECT of LIFE***GENERATION GAP 42

18: ASPECT of LIFE***ECHO 44

19: ASPECT of LIFE***BALL OF COTTON 46

20: ME***TO HELL WITH MATERIALISM...47

21: ME***SPRINGTIME 49

22: ME***DOESN'T MATTER 51

23: ASPECT of LIFE***A SMILE AND A SCOWL! 52

24: ME***THE POSTMAN 54

25: ASPECT of LIFE***RETREATS...56

26: ASPECT of LIFE***WHISKERS..57

27: ME***"SUN IN AND SUN OUTSIDE".....................................58

28: ASPECT of LIFE***FLIRTING...59

29: ASPECT of LIFE***DR. JEKYLL AND MR. HYDE............................60

30: ASPECT of LIFE***MALE CHAUVINIST PIG 62

31: ME***SOJOURN OF BLISS 63

32: ME***MORE COLOURS...65

33: ASPECT of LIFE***LOVE 66

34: ASPECT of LIFE***HEAR ME OUT 67

35: ME***DECISIONS 68

36: ME***"HAPPY B'DAY" 69

37: ME***HAPPY MOTHER'S DAY 71

38: ASPECT of LIFE***CHARITY BEGINS AT HOME? 73

39: ASPECT of LIFE***MEN..75

40: ME***THOSE SMALL SENTENCES 77

41: ASPECT of LIFE***QUIET MOORINGS....................................79

42: ASPECT of LIFE***WALL..81

43: ASPECT of LIFE***DATES IN THE CALENDAR...........................82

44: ASPECT of LIFE***LAW OF THE JUNGLE................................83

45: ASPECT of LIFE***DOG HEAVEN 84

46: ASPECT of LIFE***NOVEL..85

47: ASPECT of LIFE***THE COMMON MAN 86

48: ASPECT of LIFE***JUSTICE..87

49: ASPECT of LIFE***VENDETTA...88

50: ME***A HOMEMAKER...89

51: ASPECT of LIFE***PROSTITUTION 90

52: ASPECT of LIFE***SO FAR GONE 91

53: ME***NEVER TOO LATE...92

54: ASPECT of LIFE***TO HELL WITH THE WORD AUNTY 93

55: ASPECT of LIFE***EACH DAY 94

56: ASPECT of LIFE***ANNIVERSARIES 95

57: ASPECT of LIFE***TREES...96

58: ASPECT of LIFE***OLD AGE...97

59: ASPECT of LIFE***NO VALUE FOR VALUES 98

60: ASPECT of LIFE***PASSION, AN ESCAPE ROUTE 99

61: ASPECT of LIFE***FORGIVE AND FORGET....................100

62: ASPECT of LIFE***EXCUSES 101

63: ASPECT of LIFE***JOINT FAMILY 102

64: ASPECT of LIFE***THE BUTLER.......................................103

65: ASPECT of LIFE***DIFFERENT 104

66: ME***ANGELS 105

67: ASPECT of LIFE***EMPATHY 106

68: ASPECT of LIFE***THE APPLE...107

69: ASPECT of LIFE***CLAQUE...108

70: ASPECT of LIFE***CEMETERY 109

71: ME***OF YORE..110

72: ME***'THE DIE-HARD'..111

73: ASPECT of LIFE***HOLDING HANDS...............................112

74: ME***THAT HUMAN CONNECT.......................................113

75: ME***PASSION 114

76: ME***CHANGING OF TRACKS 115

77: ME***CHRISTMAS 116

78: ME***GERMANY 117

79: ME***BEYOND 118

80: ASPECT of LIFE***CHARITY 119

81: ASPECT of LIFE***THE RED CARPET 120

82: ASPECT of LIFE***LOST MOMENTS 121

83: ME***U.S.A./AMERICA..122

84: ME***THE BRUNETTES...123

85: ME***THE FRENCH 124

86: ME***THE STIFF-UPPER-LIPPED.....................................125

87: ME***OH! THOSE HINDI CLASSES 126

88: ME***WAS IT?..127

89: ASPECT of LIFE***FEELINGS...128

90: ASPECT of LIFE***THE GHOST WRITERS.................................129

91: ME***IN BIHAR...130

92: ME***THESE GREY HAIR...131

93: ME***AN 'EMOTIONAL FOOL' . . . TO BE RECKONED WITH ...132

94: ME***A REVERIE...133

95: ME***FACEBOOK..134

96: ASPECT of LIFE***SPARING OF NONE 135

97: ASPECT of LIFE***AT ONE'S NAKED BEST 136

98: ASPECT of LIFE***THE TRAIN JOURNEY 137

99: ASPECT of LIFE***THE BARTENDER.......................................138

100: ASPECT of LIFE***BEYOND CONTROL 139

101: ME***OH THIS ADDICTION 140

102: ASPECT of LIFE***TO BE OR NOT TO BE . . . ? 141

103: ASPECT of LIFE***FASHION...142

104: ASPECT of LIFE***SMALL WONDERS 143

105: ASPECT of LIFE***THE OTHER SIDE OF THE FENCE 144

106: ASPECT of LIFE***BALANCE...145

107: ASPECT of LIFE***THE LULLABIES..146

108: ASPECT of LIFE***HANGERS 147

109: ASPECT of LIFE***PROPERTY...148

110: ASPECT of LIFE***THE INTRINSIC TRUTH............................149

111: ASPECT of LIFE***OH! THIS HANDKERCHIEF 160

112: ASPECT of LIFE***THE GUESS GAME....................................161

113: ASPECT of LIFE***HAPPINESS..162

114: ASPECT of LIFE***TRINITY..163

115: ASPECT of LIFE***THE GOSSIP MONGERS 164

116: ME***MY MUMMY IS FOREVER..165

117: ME***THE ABSENCE—OR IS IT?...166

118: ASPECT of LIFE***TIME...167

119: ASPECT of LIFE***SELF-IMAGE...168

120: ASPECT of LIFE***MATCH FIXING..169

121: ME***LEGACY OF WISDOM 171

122: ME***THE WOMEN OF BIHAR 173
123: ME***LOVE AND PASSION..175
124: ASPECT of LIFE***SILENCE 176
125: ME***THANK YOU PAPA 177
126: ASPECT of LIFE***CAKE-WALK? 179
127: ME***MY WRITINGS? 180
128: ME***IN QUANTUM MOTION..181
129: ME***THE MOON 183
130: ME***MIDSUMMER NIGHT...184
131: ME***A TAIL?..185
132: ME***BED OF ROSES 186
133: ME***CHOOSY..187
134: ASPECT of LIFE***HATS 188
135: ME***ICE SALT..189
136: ASPECT of LIFE***PUT ASIDE EVERYTHING 191
137: ASPECT of LIFE***GREETINGS...193
138: ME***FRIENDSHIP..194
139: ASPECT of LIFE***RACE 195
140: ME***HOTCHPOTCH 196
141: ME***WHAT'S THERE IN A NICKNAME? 198
142: ASPECT of LIFE***NARCISSISM 200
143: ASPECT of LIFE***NAMELESS..202
144: ME***ALCOHOL 203
145: ASPECT of LIFE***THE GOLDEN SPOON....................................205
146: ASPECT of LIFE***ROOTS 206
147: ME***AT THE END...208
148: ASPECT of LIFE***CONSCIENCE 209
149: ASPECT of LIFE***CONTRASTS 210
150: ME***A MEDLEY 211
151: ME***THE TWINKLE EYED DELIGHTS...213
152: ASPECT of LIFE***SMILE...214
153: ASPECT of LIFE***RHYTHM 215
154: ME***A SHADOW 216

155: ASPECT of LIFE***MONEY..217

156: ASPECT of LIFE***BEAUTY AND BRAINS...................................218

157: ASPECT of LIFE***SOMETIMES...219

158: ASPECT of LIFE***SEXUAL FAVOURS..................................220

159: ME***PASSIONATE MADNESS..221

160: ASPECT of LIFE***EDUCATED OR LITERATE.......................222

161: ME***I AM SORRY..223

162: ME***FOR NO FAULT OF MY DEAR HUSBAND.....................224

163: ASPECT of LIFE***TO EARN..226

164: ASPECT of LIFE***THE DWARFED WORLD 227

165: ASPECT of LIFE***IF ONLY..228

166: ME***WALL-FLOWER..229

167: ASPECT of LIFE***EMPATHISE.......................................230

168: ASPECT of LIFE***'LE DINER'..231

169: ASPECT of LIFE***'LA CHIME'...232

170: ASPECT of LIFE***FAIR WEATHER FRIENDS....................233

171: ASPECT of LIFE***THE STIFF UPPER LIPPED....................234

172: ASPECT of LIFE***GROUNDED.......................................235

173: ASPECT of LIFE***SOCIAL BUTTERFLIES.........................236

174: ASPECT of LIFE***THE IN-LAW SYNDROME......................237

175: ASPECT of LIFE***MIKE CLINGERS.................................238

176: ASPECT of LIFE***CASANOVAS......................................239

177: ASPECT of LIFE***VISITING 240

178: ASPECT of LIFE***RAISING A TOAST 241

179: ASPECT of LIFE***ART...242

180: ASPECT of LIFE***ELITES AND PROLETERIATS.................243

181: ME***IN LOVE...244

182: ASPECT of LIFE***THE CHRISTMAS TREE........................245

183: ME***YOUR CALLING...246

184: ASPECT of LIFE***ACCEPTANCE 248

Poems

1: TO BE IN SYNC..251

2: BALANCE..252

3: POTION...253

4: SWIIIIIIIIIIIIIIIIISH!...254

5: FASHION...255

6: MARRIAGES..256

7: LOVE IN THE POCKETS....................................257

8: NOT BORN A PRINCESS...................................258

9: MOMENTS..259

10: ME..260

11: VAGABOND..261

12: NIGHTINGALE...262

13: HOLDING HANDS..263

14: AMEN...264

15: ONENESS...265

16: BEAUTY...266

17: OH!..267

18: MOODINESS..268

19: AS I AM..269

20: PETTICOAT GOVERNMENT.........................270

21: CHARITY..271

22: COMPULSIVE TALKERS...............................272

23: BEAUTY AND BRAINS...................................273

24: SHE..274

25: SMALL JOYS...275

26: "YES BOSS"...276

27: PASSION..277

28: BUNCH OF CRIMSON JOY............................278

29: SOMERSAULT...279

30: HONOUR...280

31: GOSSIP MONGERING 281
32: SHADOWS AND WHISPERS 282
33: REAL FROM THE UNREAL 283
34: ALONE 284
35: CHANGE 285
36: COFFIN 286
37: CELEBRITY 287
38: CHIEF GUEST 288
39: CHAIR 289
40: MUMMY 290
41: PAPA 291
42: MEN 292
43: OPEN DOOR 293
44: ENIGMA 294
45: NRI 295
46: SELFISH MODE 296
47: THE FAIRY WORLD 297

Acknowledgements

My deep appreciation to Partridge Publishing for bringing my work to light and to my editor, Surojit Mohan Gupta, for helping me put it together.

Dedication

In the fond memory of my parents,
Papa and Mummy
***
Dedicated to my family:
My husband, Madhukar, and sons,
Anurag and Vinamra
***
Inspired by,
An Anonymous 'Shadow'

Author's Note

The book *RANDOM THOUGHTS* is a compilation of write-ups, on those aspects of life I have felt and feel strongly about. Nostalgic reflections as I move down memory lane, reminiscing about the bygone days, sometimes with childish glee, sometimes with remorse and at other times with a hopeful hope. The writings likewise are a smooth blend of the past merging into the present and vice-versa.

I write with candour, which most oft than not verges on to bluntness since I write straight from the heart, a sort of umbilical connect betwixt my thoughts and words. Words have an intangible power of coming alive, like a painting on a canvas, making the reader get lost amidst their folds.

Random Thoughts I hope will give respite to the readers from the day-to-day stresses of life as they will traverse through the journey of my life with a keen involvement and interest. The writings were penned betwixt May 2012 and March 2014.

Thank you.

Jesus Christ . . . in whose love and faith
I have surrendered my life.
Amen . . . !!!

1: ME***IN THE WOODS

She stood, alone and lost, in the woods, bewildered. Her eyes met the fallen leaves, once so beautiful and to be trampled upon now. She picked that stray rose and a thorn pricked her, tears welled up in her eyes, "Why, I did no wrong?" That cosy nest, the baby birds, so snug and safe, in there will be out on their own soon, fending for themselves. She looked around for a way out, as she wearily moved on and suddenly she espied two paths before her leading out of the wood. The shorter path was laden with flowers on both the sides but the end of the path seemed so bleak and dead. The longer path, though not so full of radiance at the start, was blessed with a myriad of flowers, as though laughing and swaying with the breeze at the far end. Inadvertently she started walking on the longer path, a pebble hurt her foot, she knew there would be many more but she cared not. Her lineage, her parents' boundless love, her upbringing and her education, put their arms around her, like her guardian angels and she moved on, moved on with her life fearlessly. Exams after exams, par excellence, met her confident gait and each time she heaved herself up. She smiled for she knew, the wood was far behind her now. For she knew, her smiles would lend their radiance to the flowers, at the end of the road.

2: ME***WHERE HAS IT GONE?

It's strange how the spirit gets kindled or dies out, making its presence or absence felt, in the manner of one's gait, according to the ever changing situations in one's life. I can so vividly visualise my running footsteps on the stairs leading to the veranda of my home in Lucknow, when my parents were there. Their excitement at my coming no lesser than mine, with me rushing into their outstretched arms, our fond waiting to be together, culminating into a huge, warm hug. The warmth of that one small gesture, saying it all. The sprightliness in my walk, as I went around doing those little caring acts for their comfort, not to be lacking in any way, for the small time that I would be there. Returning from shopping and rushing up again to strew everything around, for them to see.

With my mother also no longer now, waiting to encircle me in her loving arms, my legs feel heavy like lead, as I climb up the steps and make my way to our rooms there. It takes me a while to enter, as I halt at the threshold, desperately trying to hold back my tears of ever such fond memories. Weakly I tip-toe in and with quiet footsteps, walk towards the framed picture of my Papa and Mummy, on the mantelpiece and circle them in my arms, the love in no way dimmed with the passage of time, as tears gush from my eyes and I do nothing to hold them back. Where has gone the bounce from my steps? Where has gone the anticipation from my gait? Where has gone that spring in my walk? I wonder as I slowly make my way to the armchair and loose myself down the 'passage of time.'

3: ME***INTO THE MISTY HAZE

She treaded softly into the misty haze of the past . . . or into her 'wonderland' . . . and suddenly it seemed like yesterday. The fair, pretty, little, girl, running betwixt the flowers in her garden, to catch that colourful butterfly . . . her giggles wafting in the breeze. Her father's spoilt brat snuggled in his lap, feeling so loved and secure. Her demand for a pair of ballerina shoe, like all demands met in no time, and a couple of days later, the poor ballerina shoe met its fate in the garden, where it had been flung down the steps by her, simply because it had outlived her fancy. The only possession she never got tired of was her Walkie Talkie Doll, because it did exactly what she wanted it to do . . ."now say Mummy" . . ."walk now" and she would clap her hands with glee. If she landed into trouble with her cousins, which she normally did, it would take her barely a second to pull the roof down, till her father came and settled matters to her liking. Into her teens and then college, and suddenly the day of her wedding.

Walking down the aisle, holding her father's arm, little realising, that each step was taking her further away from the misty haze. That each step was bringing her closer to the harsh realities of life she was going to face. Her naivety and her honesty to be put to test at every step!

4: ME***I SAW LIFE AT THE 'GATES OF DEATH'

I saw life at the 'gates of death', I saw life, at it's naked best, at the passing away of my father and later when my mother also left for her heavenly abode. What hit me like a 'tornado', twenty-three years back, came to stay, twenty-three years later. An awakening, a realisation, at the hollowness of life, at the zero factor of life. A lifetime is spent in the pursuit of one's ambitions, a lifetime is spent in making and marring relationships, a lifetime is spent in amassing and preserving wealth, a lifetime is spent in fulfilling one's desires, and each and every minute spent hitherto, is blown off like a candle's flame . . . in the 'blink of an eye'.

I had stood transfixed, craving to see my parents, just one more time, but whoever goes never ever returns. I stood feeling dismayed at the thought that everything was just as it was, their belongings, the flowers in the garden, time ticking away at its usual pace, the sky and the stars, except my parents who had flown away from life's cage, leaving everything behind. The awareness that life is but an illusion, and we mere characters, as though come to enact our roles on life's stage, the script written at the time of conception itself, and as soon as our role gets over, the curtain comes to fall.

The ultimate truth of life, empty handed we come and empty handed we go, shook me from inside. All that we leave behind are our thoughts and actions, to be remembered with love or hatred. All their lives, my parents brought me up, instilling in me lessons about life, in their own subtle manner and even after their departure, they instilled in me the most intrinsic lesson of life, the one and only truth of life, my balustrade for life.

5: ME***"WHO SAID THIS?"

This goes back once again to my school days. Of course there were different teachers for different subjects, likewise some popular and some unpopular with the students. Nicknames of course, by the dozen . . . "Yawny" . . . "Fouly" . . . "Deary" . . . and so on and so forth.

Our Maths was taken by a Sir and Algebra and Geometry by a Miss in Christ Church College. The Maths teacher was a drone and a bore and in no time would I start yawning or fidgeting, waiting for the Maths period to get over as fast as possible. The Miss was a sprightly, young lady who meant business, the moment she clipped-clopped on her pencil heels into the class and started rolling off problems, as though she knew them at her finger tips.

During one such Maths class our Sir got stuck with a Maths problem and took an unusually long time trying to solve it on the blackboard. I could feel my patience wearing out and apprehended it would get the better of me in no time. Suddenly I heard my voice "Sir shall I call Miss X to solve the problem?" (Meaning of course our Algebra and Geometry teacher.) There was a pin-drop silence as he turned around and glared at the class from above his specs, as was his habit, and hollered "Who said this?" Undaunted I replied "Me Sir . . ." "I knew it would be you. Who else will have the cheek to speak like this?" As I stood in my place I knew what was going to follow. The peon was summoned and I was packed off to the Principal's office with a note from Sir.

Once again a scolding of a lifetime and sent back was I to class, which to my glee I was not allowed to enter, as a mode of punishment. What did I do in the meanwhile? I made my way towards the end of the corridor, from where I could have a lovely view of the forbidden mangoes hanging from the trees and my mind went a racing and planning, as to how many mangoes would I somehow make my hands full with, the coming day?

6: ME***PAPER BALLS

Many a times we fail to assess our own potential, till others start talking about it. Many a times we have false assumptions of our potential, till others start talking about it and many a times we have no clue to our hidden potential, till by a quirk of fate, it jumps into the limelight. I fall into the latter category.

Of course, as a teenager I used to simply scribble poems and my thoughts, just for the heck of it. Roll them into 'paper balls' and either whisk them away into the waste paper basket or throw them at my siblings or cousins and the more their annoyance the more I would love that 'paper ball', loving it not for what was written in it. These writings continued to be thus worthlessly rolled into 'paper balls', till many years back I flattened one out, got it typed and posted the same to the *Statesman*, Calcutta. Lo and behold, there was a letter informing me about it's approval for publication. I was flabbergasted and even more so when I saw it in the paper, with my name and an illustration of 'My Father's Armchair'. Followed a quick succession of publication of nearly eight articles in their column 'Now and Again'. Then somehow my problems got the better of me and my writing got shelved. My parents would keep persuading me to take up my pen again but somewhere that spirit to write had vanished.

It was a few months after my mother's passing away and that unbearable vacuum in my life, made me hold my pen again in May 2012. Thanks to the Facebook wall, my thoughts once again started to flow into words and then came my 'blog' my 'niche'. My 'paper balls' became my passion, my means of catharsis, as I kept writing relentlessly, unharnessed, blind to the reactions of the readers. Today I can no longer motivate myself to roll them into 'paper balls' because somewhere I have come to realise my 'calling' . . . what if it took its birth in the form of 'paper balls'. Still I know 'I have miles to go before I sleep and miles to go before I sleep.'

7: ME***THE WILD BERRY

Hindi, of course, was my best subject in school, with me getting the highest marks in it. Never an exam did go by without a red mark under the subject Hindi, spoiling the entire look of my report card. Despite that putting my head to it for more than fifteen minutes, well was like putting my head inside a bucket of hot water. I used to get that queasy feeling in my head, which I get even today, when in the throes of my temper, though my temper is much on the ebbing end now.

There is a wild berry with thorns which most of you, I'm sure, must have found, sticking to the tails of cattle and goats. Well, if it gets into your hair, the latter gets so badly knotted up with the berry, there's no way out but to cut off that strand of hair in order to get rid of it. I had espied quite a few of them, waving out to me, while strolling in the rear grounds of my school. One fine day an idea struck my mind and picking a couple of them, did I boast in front of my friends "Just wait and see, what I'm going to do today?"

Home-time bell went ringing 'Ding-Dong' and I went running to the gate, for I knew my Hindi teacher would be waiting there for her vehicle and sure enough she was. I went towards her back and picking up one of those wild berries from the front pocket of my school bag, thrust it, nice and proper in her huge hair-bun. Smilingly thinking to myself "Today when she combs her hair, she'll remember all the red-marks she's beautified my report cards with." It was sooner thought than realised because as I was making my way away, I suddenly found my ear tweaked and taken was I to the Principal's office by her. I later got to know how a girl who was labelled as 'tattler-tit' had seen me in action and had promptly reported it to her.

What followed was of course history, with the letter of being expelled from school, sent to my father and how he managed to handle my Principal, he alone knew. Little did I have the maturity to understand then that all the red-marks were due to my fault and not hers. She was doing her duty as a teacher whereas I was not doing mine as a student and tried taking out my frustration by sticking that wild berry into her bun.

After coming out of the Principal's office, in spite of a good dressing down, I can recall thinking to myself "O.k. Miss lay your hands on your comb today and remember me as much as you can, for neither will you set yourself right and nor will I." Even today if I happen to see that wild berry, it never fails to evoke a smile on my face.

8: ME***ALWAYS BY MY SIDE . . .

Time tip-toes by without your realising how quietly the present has gone into the past, each day a storehouse of emotions and experiences, always there to be delved into, as and when.

Last night I turned sides, as it dawned on me, that its almost close to a year since Mummy left for the other realm. The pain as intense, the feel of her as close, the last togetherness as vivid and the final goodbye as heart-tearing, as it had been a year back.

Despite Mummy's physical absence never ever did I feel, she's not around. Her voice I could always hear, encouraging me, scolding me, pacifying me, as and when. The tender feel of her caresses, as she wiped my tears, shed in privacy, gave that comforting squeeze to my hand when needed, guided me whenever I found myself standing at a cross-road, unable to decide which way to go, the sound of her confident footsteps, brushing mine, always there. Her resounding laughter at my happiness as welcoming as mine.

So innumerable years will breathe by but never will I be bereft of my parents' selfless love, their presence by my side, loving me, propelling me, their legacy, never at a loss. Me as I stand today, a part of their wholesome being, as they moulded me together forever and forever.

9: ME***THE SUNNY DREAMS

As I reclined in my armchair after a hard day's work, my mind completely relaxed from the day's chores, I found my heavy eyelids closing and my mind started to drift away, I think into that realm which is just a few footsteps away from the real world, into the wishful world of dreams, not the dreams we see in our sleep but the dreams known as 'daydreams'. My mind was as though racing to outwit one wish after another, wishes toppling over each other for their fulfilment. The only thing lacking was a fairy's wishing wand, with all its sparkle of stars.

Ah! The great feel of my novel, finally complete and published, all my thoughts blissfully compiled, for generations to swear by, ready to be launched. There I stood with my usual becoming and confident demeanour (of course it mattered not, how many butterflies were making their rounds in my tummy) giving a small talk on what had inspired me to pen the book, and it's breathing essence. Tears almost rolled down my cheeks, at the applause. Oh! The day I had waited for all my life was finally mine for asking, my thrill knew no bounds.

Suddenly I was pulled down from the clouds of heaven, as the screeching sound of the call-bell hurt my ear drums. Painfully I dragged open my eyes to see nothing better but plain sheets of papers, strewn around me, flying here and there, like my thoughts. My pen limply held betwixt my fingers, as though waiting to autograph the first copy of my published book. A book written and lost in the 'day dreamer's realm of nought'.

10: ME***TO BE CONVINCED

I truly have to be convinced about any issue before I can change my mind. I have used the words "can be made to change my mind" because nothing on earth can make me look the other way, if I want not to. Getting convinced doesn't mean, a long list of the plus and minus has to be shown to me, for then will I get so embroiled as to refuse to budge, like a mule, from where I am standing. My conviction comes on it's own. How my thought process falls into that slot I have never tried to pragmatically analyse and will venture to do so, now, as my fingers keep moving on the key board.

It's probably got a lot to do with my sixth sense or my gut instinct, which happens to be pretty paramount. It's not as though it's always at my beck and call, it comes like lightning to my mind and my mind is made up. Then try as much as you want to change my thought process, all efforts are going to fall flat. I hate doing something or behaving in a particular manner, simply because everyone else is doing the done thing or behaving in that manner. I have my own benchmarks to go by, benchmarks which rest on simplicity, sincerity and honesty. Uncomplicated and so easy to come by for me but decidedly not for others. Give me a million dollars and ask me to be a 'rat in the rat race', well you sure have something coming your way, by way of my 'attitude' coupled with my 'vociferous tongue'. To Hell with the million dollars, I much rather be the way I am.

Same way as nothing can make me respect or disrespect a person till I have ample reasons to do so. Position, wealth, nothing matters to me, I'll blatantly look through somebody who possesses all of these but whom I know to be a scoundrel, while the rest are busy licking his feet. A one who has nothing to his credit but character will be the recipient of all my respect and care, while the rest who treat that person like a particle of dust, can look at me askance, for all I care.

It takes me little to apologise the moment I feel that yes, I am wrong and the apology is always well meant, never lip service, can't do it at all. However ask me to apologise for no fault of mine, well then, you can sure be a witness to all Hell breaking loose.

This stubborn, mulish me is actually putty in the hands of love, compassion and genuineness and these are the facets which coupled with my gut-instincts have never failed me till date and never will.

11: ME***SING-SONG MEMORIES

I sit with my head resting on one of my arms with my fingers moving on the keyboard without anything in my mind to write upon. Generally people must be thinking how simple it is to write? Just pick up a pen and scribble away to glory. Yes! Indeed, if you wish to let your writings be a mere scribble. If not, well then, it's like the sun, moon, air and the birds and the bees joining hands to form a circle and sing "Ringa-ring o' roses . . . pocketful of posies . . . A-tishoo!, A-tishoo!, we all fall down" and down would we all go on our haunches.

Here I go with the tune and words of the innumerable games we played as kids and which seem to be ringing their welcome bells in my ears once again. "Inky, pinky, which colour do you want?" . . ."I want pink". Small, little, busy feet running amuck betwixt the blooming flower beds, looking out for that much wanted colour, pink. The ceaseless jumping in the air, waving a pink flower, as that cousin was declared the winner of that game and then once again "Inky . . . ?"

"Droom, droom" as paper pistols would wave ever so menacingly, angling for the one who couldn't save himself or herself and flat would he or she fall on the ground, as a multitude of faces, with those waving pistols, would hang over the cousin.

One of us blindfolded to play 'dark room'. Bumping here and bumping there, in the merciless effort to catch somebody, while we would hide in whichever hiding place we could, bringing in all our effort to prevent ourselves from getting caught. Finally when one did, the clapping and the shouting which accompanied the moment was such fun, as the handkerchief was removed to blindfold that cousin.

Whenever a family relative came I used to be pressed by them to sing songs from the much acclaimed movie of those days 'The Sound of Music'. There would I go with "I am sixteen, you are seventeen . . . Baby it's time to think . . ." or "So long, farewell, auf Wiedersehen goodbye . . . I hate to go and leave this pretty sight . . ." with just the right accent and the lilts and with what pride would I hear the praises and the clapping.

Years have flown by, as I try to hug those sing-song memories in my arms once again. Such small pleasures which made our lives sing and dance, to the tune of "Ringa, ringa, roses . . ."

12: ME***GAY ABUNDANCE

Do whatever you have to do, with a gay abundance, to feel the actual pulse of the moment. Whenever I laugh, my whole body laughs. That infectious gurgle in my laughter, holding on to my tummy with both my hands, tears running from my eyes, as I give myself up to the happiness of the moment. So also when I smile it's not a puckered smile but a grin which stretches from ear to ear.

When I feel the uncontrollable urge to cry, do I not? I literally howl like a babe but when there's nobody around, do I howl so. Otherwise my pillow becomes my refuge as tears flow, ever so relentlessly, coupled with my heart-rending muffled sobs, with my swollen eyes and face red like a cherry.

If pushed against the wall, does my temper really get the better of me? I actually hit back with all my might sending the other person reeling against the opposite wall (figuratively speaking). A vixen doing better justice to the term 'shrew' can never be. I'm basically a peace-loving, non-interfering person but 'all fury breaketh loose' if someone tries to unnecessarily, intentionally or maliciously spite or hurt me.

The dance floor rocks with my steps as I lose myself completely to the melody of the moment. Every bit of me attunes itself to the rhythm or the beat of the song, as I ever so gracefully waltz away to the classical numbers or whirl myself to the thumping delight of jazz songs

Lost to the world am I as my fingers go punching on the key-board, with their feathery touch and my thoughts pour out into words on the screen before me. Time as though stops, with the past, present and the future, configurating into one whole as do my heart, mind and fingers co-ordinate.

Those moments are simply made for you, when you are the Queen of those special 'tickings', to twist and turn them, to your requirements. Let yourself go or lose yourself to the beauty of those moments, with a gay abundance, filling your heart with abundant joy.

13: ASPECT of LIFE***PAST

What are memories? All that has gone into the past are termed as memories. The clock ticks 12:00 p.m. which is the present and the moment it ticks 12:01 p.m. the moment of the 12:00 p.m. has shifted into the past and the beautiful or the sad moment becomes 'was' from 'is' in a matter of a minute. Memories span far more vast an expanse than the present or the future moments.

Again with the liberty of appearing off-track, is it not heard more oft than not, "Don't keep going into your past"? Now isn't this easier said than done? It's like being asked to forget a part of your body, simply because it's become redundant now? How will you look with a part missing? It's always the cumulative effect which gives forth the true ambience. Tell me of one such person who has been able to completely disconnect from the past? I for one can't think of any to my knowledge. The conversation invariably veers into 'what was' now and then.

Little do these messiahs of sermons realise how effective the past can be? It's the best educator of the riddles of life. Absolutely no amount of reading or listening can bequeath you with the endless storage of knowledge cramped into the past days. A great uplifter of the spirit when you find it crying. Skip into those hey days and relive each moment as though now and the falling spirit will have found it's moorings of peace. Yes, the past says proudly "I am judgemental and have reasons enough to be so." It's the past which guides you regarding the handling of people and situations with which you are in the process of interacting. Just as a diamond comes forth in it's true glory with its cuttings and counter cuttings, so also does the past has the ability to keep adding treasures to your being with it's brimming moments, making you come forth with a lustre which can't be ignored.

Of course, it all depends on how much you are able to consider the worth of the past and make those moments the guiding force for your present and future. For me my most valuable casket is hidden in my past days and I do so keep peeping into them, for I know how priceless they are. Live in the present, look towards the future but never forget it's the past which will be your greatest teacher.

14: ME***RAVISHING TRESSES

Oh! Those straight long tresses of mine, my adornment, cascading my back, way down below my knees. To be plaited in school and college and to be left open to play with the breeze at evenings out. I pampered them endless when in a mood to frolic, twirled them round my fingers in annoyance when unable to have my way and showed them off to the hilt at parties and weddings.

Came marriage and the stresses along with it. My comb would cry with my laden hair, as would I. With two sons to handle and added to it my mother's-in-law never ending expectations from me, towards the household, gradually found my time creeping out of my hair management. The thought of cutting my hair short started playing on my mind, much to my parents' discomfiture and helplessness. Knowing me they had perhaps mentally prepared themselves to seeing their daughter soon with her hair clipped because it only needed that thought to make it's nest in my head.

Sure enough one fine day did I found myself walking into a parlour. "Yes Ma'am what can we do for you?" . . ."I want a hair-cut." A sceptical look flitted across the receptionist's face. "But Ma'am you have such beautiful hair." I thought one more time and will I find myself out of the door, so hurry up. "Oh! They are falling badly and so . . ." Soon was I sitting in a chair and my heart sure missed many a beat as, with a catch in my throat, did I see the scissors go "clip-clip" and my beautiful tresses I could see lying hither and thither on the floor. What a waste of all my efforts and the ravishing look of my lovely, long veil.

This story doesn't end here. A couple of years back I suddenly got a text on my mobile. "I still remember that slim, pretty, fair, nose up in the air but grounded girl in the University and can I ever forget those ravishing long hair. Anonymous admirer." I sighed "Whoever you are dear, those memorable tresses are no more. They bid adieu almost twenty years back for eternity. Thanks anyway, for remembering me ever so vividly, even after three decades." (Who this admirer was and how he got my cell number I never did try to delve into. I respect him for having remembered me so vividly despite so many years having flown by and for having had the courage eventually to speak out his heart.)

15: ASPECT of LIFE***HAPPINESS AND POSITIVITY

The easiest way to gain popularity is to talk of happiness and positivity. There are magazines, books, T.V. channels, every possible media help which handle this in their own manner. No harm. At least a genuine effort is being made for improving the quality of the life of us humans. However at the cost of appearing cynical, I have my own notions regarding all this hype over happiness and positivity.

Just rendering lip service to these attributes for making a place in the public eye or being talked of with reverence is mostly the aim. Tell me, honestly as to how many who wag their tongues in respect of happiness and positivity are in the real sense of the word, happy or positive? Maybe one in a million. This era is stress ridden making survival extremely tough, due to a lot many reasons viz., rising aspirations, disappearance of the value system, cut-throat competition and so on so forth. With this kind of an overcast sky how can anyone be expected to be happy and positive all the way? No wonder all the sages have disappeared into the Himalayas, probably finding it a waste of time banging their heads with the people in the name of happiness and positivity. Why corrupt theirs, so run to the Himalayan ranges and keep theirs intact? At least.

All this 'bla-bla' I truly look upon as merely empty talks. Negativity and unhappiness is bound to creep into in everyone's life. It's nothing unusual or to be ashamed of, since it's a natural phenomenon. No amount of external guidance or pep talks are going to be of any help. You are your biggest mentor. It's only you who can help yourself over-ride negativity, at least somewhat. To be happy in the true sense of the word is again well nigh next to impossible because happiness has different bench-marks for different people. Yes, one can have patches of a happy feel now and then.

To keep on working on it by repeating to yourself or letting empty words fall in front of others "Be happy and be positive" is not going to make you budge a step, except for leaving a hollow impression on others. Lose yourself in whichever manner possible, that makes you happy your way and you'll feel that happy feeling, certainly not for eternity but definitely your life will get chequered with chunks of happiness. Silently try to calm your spirit when a negative thought enters your mind or just let it remain there and soon will it find it's way out.

This is my view of looking at happiness and positivity. I don't believe in sham, find it ever so abhorrent. Simply can't wag my tongue with words I mean not. What is public appeal going to do, if I can't appeal to myself in my own niche.

16: ASPECT of LIFE***
"WHOEVER GOES UP . . ."

Clap your hands, swing your hips, kick your legs and sing "Whoever goes up . . . Never comes back . . . Why should I break my back . . . Thinking so much so . . ." This is an attitude which has struck a million over like an epidemic.

Everything is justifiable, everything is commendable, there is nothing that can be otherwise, simply act and do whatever comes into your head. Lie, steal and borrow but meet your ends. Wear a mask all the time, leave alone the others, very soon will you forget which is the real you. Satisfy your carnal needs, under wraps or on a bench in the park, then why call a dog a dog and a bitch a bitch. The sanctity of a marriage's sanctimonious vows are confined to the altar only, which makes me wonder as to why the Pastors take all the trouble of pronouncing them, a well meaning effort which gets shelved at the drop of a hat. Cling to a person like bees, so long the going is good and run for your life the moment a hurricane attacks the person, to weather the pelting of the hailstorm alone, whose feet you have been licking for uncountable evenings of booze or whatever.

The words 'ethics and values' have become clichés or non-existent. Why waste time and energy over such block-busters when everything is at your beck and call, by simply standing with your back towards the integrity of your character? Why muzzle over misgivings when you can have none because you have put your conscience to rest.

Holler at the top of your voice "Whosoever goes up . . ." but towards the end of your journey of life, will all your thoughts and acts engulf you like multitude of shadows, mocking and sneering at you. Everyday will rewind like a camera reel, as will you smother sob after sob, but will there be anyone around to render you that much needed respite? No because you whiled away that precious life at the mercy of your whims and fancies, caring not, indulging in everything possible to quickly meet the need of the hour, anyhow.

Tis a fact "Nobody who goes . . ." and where stands the need to, when you get repaid more than amply, while you are still breathing your last and desperately praying for His mercy, which will elude you then, in the same manner as you did, all that was good.

17: ASPECT of LIFE***GENERATION GAP

Today while talking to a friend of mine from Delhi, her adult daughter took the mobile and did I find myself dumbstruck with many of her contentions, so much so, I was at a loss for words at times. Little do we make an effort to understand the way others think, so caught up are we with our own mental set-up. The thin wedge soon becomes a gaping hole, with both hanging onto their strings, not willing to take that first step of "O.K. I'll try to understand your feelings."

"We get to live once and if we are not able to live the way we want, what is the use?" . . ."My mother has to learn to let go. Do the birds keep flying after their young ones. They fly off on their own, as soon as they are able to?" I tried arguing with her about the pressures on her mother and if she interfered it was for her good, after all she was still not on her own, to which smack came the retort "We all have her pressures but I don't keep harassing her with mine. I handle them my way. Half the time she doesn't even know what I'm undergoing." Could I say anything to this and told her as much "Ya I agree with you."

This is what is called 'generation-gap'. Each have their defences to be thrown, as and when and each defence comes hurtling back with a greater force. Times are fast changing at every step, 'with what was not' has now become 'with what is', what with the younger generation becoming more and more wayward.

Elders have their own yardsticks and youngsters have theirs. An extremely conflicting scenario, whereby none thinks the other wiser than oneself and when two wise heads meet there are bound to be fire-works. Fire-works only with none trying to extinguish it and the third person can at best lend a well meaning ear to both but certainly can't bring harmony. Maybe for that little time but to give fast roots to this harmony both the generations will have to stand in each other's shoes and this seems like well nigh next to impossible.

I always thank Him for small mercies. I have been blessed with two adult sons but never can I recall us coming to a clash. It goes both ways viz., both have a strong sense of respect for elders, are absolutely undemanding, grounded, with a very strong sense of values. As a mother I find myself detached only to the extent that they have their own lives to live, why should I unnecessarily keep poking my nose. I am too confident of the way I have brought up my boys and render my advice only when it's sought or the few times when I have thought it imperative to render it at my discretion and leave it to them to adhere to it or not.

To be judgemental is not my business, the least I can do is to express my views and the rest is up to the others. I have a right over my life and not on anyone else's. At least I have the good sense to genuinely feel the hurts of others and do the little I can, by whichever means, to give them the much needed solace. If things keep moving in the direction they are, well then 'God save the King', both the generations will be at each other's neck, the parents, parents only in name and the children, children only in name. None around to lend that much needed shoulder in times of need.

18: ASPECT of LIFE***ECHO

Life is an echo. Whatever you say, do or think comes back to you, either in equal measure or for the better or the worse, but it decidedly does. I can vouch for it from my own experiences in life and from my observant, keen senses as I allow them to roam around, gathering rudiments from the lives of others.

Do good and good will be seen marching down your pathway. The manner in which you get repaid will of course be different but the handshake will never be missed out upon. Do bad, and some misfortune will be found lurking at the corner, a reminder of your unfortunate deed.

All our actions are the resulting factor of our thoughts. It's the positive or negative thoughts which culminate into our doings. These wave lengths are the measuring yardsticks for our behavioural pattern. To say that the thoughts will always be positive is well nigh next to impossible. However an effort can always be made to 'nip them in the bud', though it's easier said than done but no harm in trying. With me it's a lot different. I have a very pungent 'gut instinct' and can weigh the character of a person from miles off and well then I stay away if my hunch tells me to. The reason, why I am termed a snob, in general. To be honest I am not a snob at all, it's just that I become stiff with those who have put me off even before they got a chance to talk to me and believe me, so far I have never found myself wanting, then does my mind refuse to peep that side. This way the chance of any kind of negativity towards anyone, weighing me down, becomes non-existent like the person. This instinct surely must have been dormant in me, to have made its presence felt, as I treaded on the cobbled aisles of my life.

There are innumerable queries which used to jostle my mind, now and then. Why do bad things happen with good people or why do the not so good ones are more happy in life? Till now I have never come across anyone who has been able to give a concrete answer, they simply take you on a merry-go-round ride, to find yourself eventually standing in the same square from where you started.

I have just stopped bothering my head over questions which seem more like riddles. The only placard which gazes at me, un-blinkingly is . . . yes, life is an echo . . . endeavour to let the echo come back to you . . . with a melody sweeter than the one you sent forth . . . an echo which will be there resonating in your ears . . . when you bid your last farewell.

19: ASPECT of LIFE***BALL OF COTTON

Everyone is born naked, so amazingly pure in this nakedness, bereft of any strapping. A free soul, soon to be bonded. Like a drop of water from the vast ocean which finds itself suddenly but lovingly clasped in the bosom of a shell, swimming with the tides journey, no longer just a drop in the ocean. A pretty pearl now, giving it a feel of belonging and from here starts the saga of its life. The moment you cry your first into this world, one after another the baggage start to pile on. The arms holding you in that loving cradle are your Mom's, that proud face peeping from behind is your Dad's, that little boy throwing a tantrum to kiss you is your brother and so and so forth. Your small, little body has already got attached to relationships, you are unaware of.

Soon a list is prepared with names hunted from all over the world and you are given a name, with no say in it whatsoever, for eternity. A name which you spontaneously accept since you have no option but to. This name becomes your so called identity in every wake of life, and then it's left to you to make the most of it or to lump it.

A religion is already hovering over the cradle to make its presence felt to perfection.

The little spider has taken its first step into the cobweb. Gradually with ever such silent steps the initial nakedness starts to cover itself bashfully with clothing, one after another, or the small free shoulders begin to get weighed down with baggage which keeps mushrooming faster than mushrooms.

The small ball of cotton, still lost in the smiles and tears of its dreams, even before it has learnt to turn sides, even before it has learnt to utter a syllable, is harnessed with uncountable pieces of baggage, so heavy for its tender shoulders.

20: ME***TO HELL WITH MATERIALISM

Come to think of it, I never hanker after material assets. I'm more than contented with whatever much or little I have and never ashamed or embarrassed about what I don't have. Now this is not as simple as it comes forth apparently on the surface. There's a huge pile of analysis behind this indifferent attitude towards things on a material level.

I had the privilege of being born into a prestigious, affluent family of Lucknow. Right from the time I was just that little, big enough, I remember growing up in luxury and comfort. Never did have to shake my little finger for anything, except of course for studying, which took its toll on my parents due to my playing truant all the time. I can never recall my parents sitting and sermonising but everything was being wonderfully inculcated into my being by my parents balanced lifestyle and despite my being pampered to the hilt by my father, I used to shake like a leaf when he was affronted by me, which was more oft than not. His authoritative tone would make me cower for cover. Having grown up breathing in an environment of abundance, with my parents tweaking my ears, now and then when found trespassing my limits, made me satiated with material benefits and inculcated in me the real worth of money. Just that much of importance to it and not an iota beyond. My father's sentence has its hold over me, even today "When you start speaking money, then that money has lost its worth."

My schooling in Loreto Convent and subsequently in Christ Church further enriched my character, adding depth and wealth by way of literacy, mannerisms, values and a liberated thought process, all of which went hand in hand with my parents grooming.

Added to all this was my education of life vide my tribulations, happenings, people I came in contact with, either willingly or unwillingly, my sensitive observations. Always gathering some experience, making me wiser than what I was a day earlier, more and more getting to understand how temporal materialism is.

This contentment thus has a great deal of backing, which lies hidden in my past. My strength, my boldness, my bluntness, my candidness, my nonchalant attitude, all have their bearings in these piles which only I can fathom. A big minus factor which I perceive in myself is my arrogance, related to my lineage. However it rears its head only when I feel its necessity to do so. I never, ever flaunt my arrogance to demean anyone. Could I have boasted of the same 'Me' had circumstances in my life been different? I really can't vouch for it but in all probability 'No'.

21: ME***SPRINGTIME

Springtime is in the air. A harbinger of musical notes around, that moist, body clinging, sweet fragrance hanging in the air, the cherry like baby buds blossoming into flowers, birds ever so busy building their nests and me with that song "Lots of chocolates for me to eat . . ." on my lips.

The cuckoo bird's infectious cuckoo rants the air, the first sound which falls in my ears as I lazily open my eyes to a new day. With a wistful look do I see a sweet, little girl standing in the garden and mimicking them "cuooooooo" and back comes the sound "cuooooooo" followed by the gurgling laughter and the clapping of the hands, as does her wandering gaze look around to see the owner of this air-renting sound, emanating from amidst the foliage of the trees. The little girl disappearing into the folds of my memories as the calls of the day beckon me to their side.

What is the use of the Arabian perfumes, their fragrance trapped in corked exquisite bottles, to be rendered on those special evenings? I can feel my nostrils tingle to the sensation of an unmatched fragrance as though travelling through the gamut of expansive surroundings around. Unmatched, so sweet in its virgin feel, as though aspiring to entice me with its tender feel.

The buds so chaste and secure, as though bashfully uncovering their hitherto hidden beauty to the passerby's admiring gaze, letting go, as each petal unfolds itself with the coyness of a bride. Let them frolic and flirt with the winsome breeze, let not anyone trespass on their secret, virgin moments. Bless them and go by.

The twittering birds, ever so busy with a single minded purpose, go flitting from the ground to the safety of the trees, with dried grass in their beaks, to build their nests. Soon will they lay their eggs in the soft cradle, to be hatched into "Oh" such heart warming little ones. Opening their red beaks with a musical clamour, as they climb over one another to get their share of the morsel from their Mom's beak. A sight so captivating for that chirpy, naughty girl, who yearned to hug them to her cheeks but dared not, remembering her father's words "If you'll touch the little ones, their parents will abandon them and go". A smile played on my lips as her retaliation played in my ears "but you and Mummy don't abandon me, when someone pulls my cheeks, though it hurts so", as did I feel my father's warm hug once again, stretched over years.

Spring which ushers in a babe like freshness to the tune of the "cuoooooo" lilting in the dewy air, with the bridal veil of the flowers as though falling apart to the melody and the romance in the springtime around, with an impish look now and with a mellowed look then, do I become a rollicking soul, with the springtime around.

22: ME***DOESN'T MATTER

Have been described very aptly lately by my men friends. A few days back one called me "archaic" and today another friend said "You are so clear hearted, as to be termed foolish in today's times". Now both of them have known me pretty closely since 'donkey years'. There definitely must be some iota of truth in their thus assessment of me.

How did I feel in being categorised as 'archaic' and 'foolish'? None endearing terms. I simply smiled both the times without making the effort to justify myself. Why? Both of them are very close to my heart and I respect them for having the strength to speak their minds out to me always, whenever, and whatever they say is always backed by honesty and good intentions, never a touch of malice or with linings of trying to demean me. Now had these observations stemmed from malafide intentions, I would have let my steam out in a manner entirely my own. I can be quite a vixen if I find somebody endeavouring to unnecessarily 'rub me the wrong way' and it's then I find myself striking back with all my might.

Nothing fell on 'deaf ears'. Once again my mind went a ticking and I found a good deal of truth in what they had said. 'Archaic' I am regarding my manner of viewing life with all my sense of values and morals, which hold no meaning for people nowadays. There are other things much more important than sticking to hackneyed stuff but for me the guiding force. 'Foolish' I am again if measured by the yardsticks of this century. To be an 'open book' is certainly smirked at today. Knowing myself I'll stifle to death if I allow layers to freeze over my heart and mind. To undergo that kind of claustrophobia is beyond me to cope up with, too much of an effort to come by.

Let me be 'archaic', let me be 'foolish'. At least I have the strength to be 'me' with all my plus and minus . . . proud of my virtues . . . if not proud of my failings, at least not ashamed . . . to be able to walk with my head held high . . . not shying away from anyone's gaze . . . no matter what the position be of the person . . . for what holds my regard is how one comes across as a human being and not the peripherals.

23: ASPECT of LIFE***
A SMILE AND A SCOWL!

A man once happened to meet a 'genii'. The 'genii' told the man to ask for a wish. The latter shook his head, this way and that way, then with a big smile said "Please make a bridge betwixt the earth and Heaven." The genii replied "Well this is next to impossible. Ask me for something else." The man did ponder for a while and then made his second wish "O.K. What is it which will keep a woman happy?" Now was it the turn of the 'genii' to shake his head, this way and that way and after much thought the 'genii' said "I will grant you your first wish." Such is the consensus about women.

It's easier to climb up to the highest peak of the Himalayas, it's well within reach to attain your cherished goal, no matter how out of reach it may seem but to please a woman is well nigh next to impossible. No matter what the men folks may do, they will always be finding themselves falling short. Present her with a villa, she'll hanker for a mansion. Gift her a Rolls Royce and after a while she'll ask you to give her a ride in a better car and if there's none, well then invent a new one to suit her fancy. This goes for the elites and the women of the middle class go by what is the latest trend by way of fashion, the neighbour's material assets and all that it takes to project a 'glitzy' image of oneself in their kitties and what have you. All of these of course keep somersaulting, as and when but surely faster than the high and the low tides.

The poor men keep slogging day in and day out, to cater to the women's capricious demands, trying desperately to keep frantic pace with the changing 'mood scenarios', endeavouring their level best to see that happy smile on their faces last. All for a lark. "Oh! Can there be a better person than you", as you stand with that precious gift, a huge grin on your face and in a matter of two days "Oh! You never know what I want?" Opening and closing your mouth like a goldfish, do you start to wonder as to what has gone wrong, where?

The 'genii' didn't shake his head without reason and eventually backed out when asked about what can keep a woman happy? She is a rare phenomenon beyond the understanding of all. Utterly unpredictable and whimsical, always wanting what is not, her benchmarks never her own but always at the disposal of the assets of others, her mood swings so rapid as to turn a "cutie-pie" into a "Hitler" in a matter of seconds. Dear men, no matter how superior you may think yourself to the fair sex, this surely is one area in which you will always find yourself completely at bay. You can get the stars from the sky, still will you never, ever be able to make a woman happy, not only in this lifetime but in all the future ones as well.

24: ME***THE POSTMAN

Birds and animals are getting extinct and added to this list are the postmen. As though a dwindling history but never to be shelved into the dusty shelves of bygone days by me. How can they be? Always a harbinger of the much awaited letters from my family in Lucknow.

With what joyous abundance would I look forward to those inland letters from my parents and my sisters. Feelings, emotions, missing out, advices as and when, would come pouring out the moment I used to slit them open with the excitement of a child. The letters, absorbing my grins, my laughter, my sniffles and my tears. How those pearl like drops would drop, smudging the ink here and there. Every bit written to me, never giving me an opportunity to complain or throw a fit, as to why such and such a thing was kept away from me. Many a times my arms would hug those sharings, as would I get lost in their always warm, cuddly and beckoning arms. An unexplainable respite from the arduous journey I was treading on.

My pen moving ever so restlessly, unable to keep momentum with the upsurge of my emotions and longing to be within the loving folds of my family, now so many miles away. Trials written in anger and then scratched to prevent my family from undergoing any kind of pain. My heart ripping apart and many a moments when their spoilt daughter's tears would smudge the paper and out would come another inland, for the entire matter to be re-written once again. For knowing them, I knew the smear would be immediately fathomed. My happiness, though intermittent, found it's way through my pen, now and then, resplendent with the twinkles and the chucklings. Knotted everything, the inlands like a mirage in the desert.

Thanks to the 'net' to hear the cycle bell ringing of a postman now is like something 'out of the blue' yet despite the faraway time, it still never fails to give me a welcome jolt, as I crumble inside with the lost feeling, for whose letter shall I wait now, for whose love and warmth residing in every alphabet, shall I wait now, for both my parents are no more, that binding force is broken? All that remains and, come to think of it, a lot remains by way of all those tender emotions tied together with a blue ribbon, the paper so brittle yet the feel so treasured, as in one of my nostalgic moments, do I read them, the years fall away, and I sit there with all their giving clutched in my arms, lost, my ears as though waiting to hear the cycle bell of the postman.

25: ASPECT of LIFE***RETREATS

Oh! These so-called 'retreats'. Leaving everything behind and scampering off to a habitat for a few days to 'realise yourself'. With all your associates back home seeing you off with that wide smile of anticipation, hoping to see you 'turn into a new leaf', after your return from this heavenly break. Little do they know?

The 'withered leaf' in the hopes of catapulting into a 'fresh green leaf' leaves bed as soon as the cock-a-doodle-doo, starting a well regimented day. Spending so called productive time in the company of learned people and all that goes in from ear, soon comes out of the other. Following to the 'T' a packed routine in a limited resources environment, much to one's annoyance but with an apparent smile. Somehow gulping down the pure, bland food served with so much love and hope. Cleaning your own room and toilet with a smiling groan. Keeping your mouth shut for a couple of hours and letting your thoughts go deep down, introspecting, retrospecting, till you feel like opening your mouth and howling like a dog. All for the benefits of self-assessment, appraisal and the subsequent 'turn over', not of a 'million dollars' but of 'the self'.

The time somehow over at the 'retreat', finds yourself groping in all your corners for that 'upliftment' but everywhere the hands seem to be as though thrown up half-way in mid-air. A month passes by, with the remnants of the little benefits hovering around you. After all some due has to be forcibly given for all the time and energy wasted. However very soon, without your realising it, you find yourself crashing head downwards in the face of the tribulations of life.

Little do you realise the futility of these stop-gap arrangements for a better you. They simply come and disappear like the vapours over an ocean. It's the education you derive on a practical, pragmatic level from the situations you have to scuffle through with in life, which are your real 'retreats'. These 'retreats' are always by your elbow . . . no martial laws to be obeyed . . . just your analysis and handling of those hiccups in life . . . to turn you into a 'fresh green leaf' . . . not only during the rainy season . . . but perennially green . . . because you have educated yourself from the nuances of life . . . an education no 'retreat' can impart.

26: ASPECT of LIFE***WHISKERS

How many spouses know exactly how the other one looks like? Living under the same roof throughout the day, day in and day out, sharing everything possible under the sky, well aware of each other's hot and cold bloodedness, in fact to a large extent, more than well familiar with all that is needed to be familiar with.

Still if you simply close your eyes and try to recollect each and every feature of the other, it'll be indeed a tough job and it's then you start feeling how much the other is taken for granted and believe me it goes either ways. Take for example the physical features, like sometime back with my husband out of station, at night my mind wandered off to the 'whiskers zone of life' and I got a jolt when my mind stubbornly refused to answer a very, very simple question viz., "Does my husband have whiskers?" The more I tried, the more it became a jig-saw puzzle for me. His face as though kept coming before my eyes, sometimes with the whiskers and sometimes sans the whiskers. What was bothering me was not so much the 'with or without' but the discomfort of the hitting realisation of the missing out on those very small yet such intrinsic crevices of life because we give not importance to those little nothings which are amongst those many pillars of life. Anyway when the door-bell rang early next morning, did I go half running and half walking to open the door. The first sentence which escaped my lips at seeing my husband was "Ah! Whiskers." He queried "What?" and I replied "Oh! Nothing really."

Come to think of it this "Oh! Nothing really" compressed in its nonchalance an integral aspect of a married life. How much or how little do you know of your partner? Are we so deeply in with the so-called essentials of life, little do we have the time nor the inclination to delve into those soft, hidden mysteries of the other, which really cost nothing but will surely add volumes to the quality of the rapport betwixt the two and will undoubtedly save the mind from the stress of finding an answer to a very mundane question "Does my husband have whiskers?"

27: ME***"SUN IN AND SUN OUTSIDE"

"Sun in and sun outside" . . . so I feel, the mornings I get out of bed with a bounce and a song on my lips. My heart dances to the thrill of my heart beat and the melody of my song makes the house swing to its lilt. The beaming light of the sun peeps in through the window panes, knocking "tuk, tuk", to let it in. As I swing the windows to usher in the sunny guest I lean my face outside, to the caressing feel of the cool, cool breeze. Out do I go running into the garden and leaning my fair face against the pink budding petals of a blooming rose, take in a deep, deep breath assimilating all the fragrance and the beauty. Aaaah! There do my eyes fall on those alluring wings of a butterfly and off I go to lay my hands on it. The giggles and the excitement as I catch it with the exuberance of yore and then with a kiss and a wish, do I let it go. The years as though washed away, once again embracing that pretty, impish girl, running hither and thither, after that butterfly with squeals of laughter and delight.

Where comes in age to nullify the wondrous feel of "Sun in and sun outside"? There is the child in everyone. Some let it remain dormant, eventually rusted with the tribulations of life, while few like me can't survive till we keep nudging and tickling it, making the child within come alive, many more times than opportunity permits.

I for sure will go jumping mad if I didn't pamper that cute, little, buoyant child in me. It makes me deliriously happy, putting to rest all my worries and bothers. Like a mirage it makes me suckle the feel of an everlasting hope and eventually the attainment of a joy forever. Nurturing an ever such a happy feel, which takes charge of that mischievous, naughty look in my eyes and waits to hear the gurgling sound of my giggles. It's all in the mind, at heart am I always sweet sixteen, with the "Sun in and sun outside".

28: ASPECT of LIFE***FLIRTING

Is flirting the privilege of only teen-agers? Oh no! It's a past-time which willingly keeps age at bay. Black hair or grey hair doesn't matter, so long you are able to have the time and the knack for flirting or are able to hang on it, even if you happen to be sweet 50+.

Fluttering eyelashes, coy eyes, that wafting giggle, revealing contours as much as can be, that 'come hither look' Ah! Sure sets a man's heart fluttering at a rate that would belie the fluttering of a bird's wings. However soon enough this 'come hither look' wears out its charm as quickly as it takes its hold and each go their way in search of their next bait, which more oft than not is lurking at the very next corner.

The men entice the women in a manner entirely their own. Chivalry at its best making the other feel no less than a princess. Compliments by the dozen till she finds herself at par with Cleopatra. That making apparent and still not making apparent of a glance as though wanting to hug her the coming minute, making her feel more wanted than his drink. Little do these stupid women realise that all this 'wanting ambience' is thanks to that intoxication which has got into his head, making his mental faculties as blurred as his speech and vision. Even if there is no drink in the hand, the compulsion to flirt is short lived, at least for the time being, at least with the same woman and in no time will she be reduced to her real self as he'll go scuttling off to find his next victim for his flirtatious need.

All my perceptions hitherto are based merely on my keen and sensitive observations. Nobody till date has had the gumption to flirt with me, probably anticipating what they'll be into, so why spoil the day and I have no regrets either because I believe not in wasting mine or the time of others on trifling things like flirting. May the flirts keep flirting to the best of their ability, if it adds spice and merriment to their lives. Who am I to complain?

29: ASPECT of LIFE***
DR. JEKYLL AND MR. HYDE

We all have two sides to us, not exactly to the extremes of Dr. Jekyll and Mr. Hyde but the boundary is the same. The personal image and the public image as I look upon it. The former is our real self, the least bit opinionated because that self is open in all its glory only to ourselves and the latter puts on an effort to propagate that cross-section of us, which will make us the darling of all whom we come across.

It doesn't take long though for a person whose intelligence is back-patted by sensitivity to look below the skin. This too is an extremely complex process in which many a things work together to be able to see the person in all his inner and outer glory as a whole. Not that something out of this world has to transpire to come down to a conclusive conclusion. Small words, gestures, reactions, body language can be eye-openers to the person's actual character. Personality is the outer aspect which is mostly manipulated to project a seemingly attractive picture to be presented before others. It can be a lot pseudo as is generally these days. The character is the real self, which is beyond human efforts to be played around with. This personality I categorise as the Dr. Jekyll and the character as Mr. Hyde.

It's indeed a rare phenomenon nowadays to come across one such who is as though an 'open book', for whom a Dr. Jekyll and a Mr. Hyde stand not to exist. To be sure, of course, if a person happens to be an 'open book' well then that one is slotted as the biggest idiot in the saga of actual idiots around. How can one not 'shoo-sha' what needs to be 'brushed under the carpet' and take the pains to paint all blossoms for those around? How can one not be smiling that blessed plastic smile and making those arms ever so long for that blessed 'bear-hug' when the other really doesn't know when the act of strangulation will take place? How can one not be a mere face in the milling crowd, to keep nodding one's head, here and there like a village bumpkin?

Worth a rat's ass all. Is it worth the magnitude of effort and energy that is squeezed in filtering what has to be added to the many 'skeletons in the cupboard' and what is to be blared? Making your ass shift from a Dr. Jekyll to a Mr. Hyde? Tossing in bed for nights or taking recourse to sleeping pills because your conscience keeps hammering you or persists in 'hanging like the Sword of Androcles over your head'?

To Hell with it all. Let me be an 'open book' . . . let me be an idiot in the eyes of those who matter to me not . . . let me sleep like a baby in the cradle, engulfed in the purity of my being . . . let that child in me ever remain . . . let Dr. Jekyll and Mr. Hyde be a part and parcel of the lives of those who have denigrated their lives to the level of a 'dime'.

30: ASPECT of LIFE***MALE CHAUVINIST PIG

Who is a 'male chauvinist pig'? A man who looks down upon every bone in a woman's body but his own. This terminology has enough to support its coming into being about a little more than half a century back.

It's not without reason that Eve was born after Adam. Since ages the balance betwixt a man's and a woman's position was taken care of, with the man as the bread-winner of the family and the woman in charge of the household. Each respected the other's position giving no cause for an earthquake to keep exploding it's lava, now and then.

Came the hurricane with the western influence infiltrating the Indian culture. Started the scenario of the women parading the streets with the slogan "I'm proud to be a woman" but with an armour in tow as well. Refusal to bow down before a man's flaunting superiority with an awareness of their newly acquired independence and the men finding their hitherto privileged position in the doldrums, goaded them to prove their muscle power with a vengeance. Surged a belligerent attitude towards one another, the balance got dis-balanced and the so called feminists landed up coining the term 'male chauvinist pig'. The pig hitherto confined to the gutters was as though suddenly thrown into the limelight.

Little are the men and women able to fathom their foolhardiness and the resulting aftermaths. The former making their muscles ripple even the more with a sadism unsurpassed and the latter trying to don the moustaches, twirling it to the best of their ability. Each bellicose towards the other, the pigs grunting with all their might and the moustaches getting longer by the day, obnoxious. Good sense having got lost somewhere betwixt the grunting and the twirling, the entire infrastructure as though gone for a lark, with none the benefactor, with none the better for the other . . . (I am not a feminist but a level headed lady who believes in giving equal due to the pigs and the borrowed moustaches but only if it is well deserved.)

31: ME***SOJOURN OF BLISS

Ever tried to let your thoughts go literally berserk? Oh! It's a feeling out of this world because when conscious of your existence, there are so many things beyond your reach but once in the clouds of imagination, you start soaring high as though amongst the clouds and the twinkling lighted ways of the stars.

I do, once in a while, when I'm free enough from the hum-drum calls of the day to day monotony. It's like being in a fairy-land with a wishing wand, which has stars and glittering speckles falling all around. There am I in Heaven, an angel with luminous wings, flying around amidst the silvery flowers and the chirping of the birds, of such ethereal beauty, as to defy imagination. Suddenly an irresistible urge to fly down and help a person who is in dire need of assistance. Within seconds, am I there and it's as though my very presence puts all the chaos to rest, as I cradle the person in my arms, throwing all the unrest to the winds and thereafter go flying back to my abode.

Driving my grandfather's Rolls Royce in a car rally and waving to the cheering crowd, with a little smile here and a little smile there, whisking past so many other cars as my surging urge to stand first keeps pumping me like fuel. Screeeeeeeeech! And there am I at the winning post, jumping and waving to the smiling, eager faces all around. The announcement 'The winner . . .' and Ah! There do I stand with the winning trophy in my hands, my smile as always stretching from one end of the ear to the other. Strangely, the disturbing feeling of the realisation that though I have won the trophy, what about all the spectators, who have been standing for hours simply to watch the winner win? What have they gained? Giving up their precious time with so much patience and love, lending their enthusiasm with such a lot of zeal, to see the winner win. My heart as though misses a beat and throwing my trophy to the winds, do I go running to the crowd and hug them with my open arms. My soul is at rest, as I reach out to them, for they are the winners in the true sense of the word.

VANDANA SINHA

With a grin am I back to this world, to its never ending demands and calls . . . but with my nerves so soothed out . . . with a feel of such utter gratification . . . because I have just made a sojourn to a world . . . so dreamy yet so true . . . filled with such loving bliss.

32: ME***MORE COLOURS

I normally like to wear muted shades, like grey, beige, white or black and the latter at one time happened to be my loved colour. Recently my sister happened to remark "Vandana, life definitely has more colours to it, than the colours which I see in your wardrobe." Sure it set my thinking prodding.

Life is a wonderful blend of hues, its range limitless, but where lies the comparison betwixt my choice of colours or the hues? Perhaps there is an underlying link. In respect of the turmoils in my post marriage days now and then, my stubborn refusal to buckle and picking up cudgels alone. Getting more and more tarnished by the day, simply because the garble of those, whom I perceived as mere specks in the milling, maddening herd, mattered to me not and hence my adamant attitude towards giving an explanation to all and sundry.

Somewhere that connect was working its way, silently and unobtrusively. My character, my personality, as though at every step was getting pruned for the better because I was subconsciously educating my being vide the hidden secrets and the truths of life. Those secrets which rear their head in everyone's life but go by unnoticed, so down till the neck are most with the shallowness and the glitz and glamour around. Added to it, maybe was my lineage, from which I have inherited a clinging taste for elegance and grace, which more oft than not, points a finger of displeasure towards anything garish, be it by way of lifestyle or demeanour.

I am aware of my wardrobe standing deprived of, what I'd call happy colours . . . not because I see life only as grey . . . and not because I'm not a happy person . . . but simply because I have been able to strike a balance . . . and my personality is a reflection . . . what if the colours in my wardrobe are grey or beige.

33: ASPECT of LIFE***LOVE

What is 'love'? It's a word beyond all realms to be able to put a finger on. An all pervasive four letter word, which lays the foundation of human existence. Nobody till today has been able to define the structure of this emotion, this feeling and never will it be defined so. How can anything which encompasses that Power, be ever restricted within folds? The little that I can vouch by way of its true essence, is of it being sublime and has to be experienced to be felt, a euphoric feel which belies all shackles and overrides it all, which condemns the human race.

Strange isn't it, how one simple emotion can project itself in a manner, entirely each to his own. The fathomless, unconditional love of parents for their children. That between spouses which verges to a large extent on the conditional. Betwixt siblings, relatives and friends which is like a see-saw and can never justify love in its purest form, always so dicey. Lovers whose love has more sexual overtures, more on the physical, than being on an emotional level. Those whose love for each other remains ever locked up in their hearts, maybe due to multifarious reasons, a love so deep, it's very feeling submerges every other aspect. That enigmatic pull towards two people for reasons unknown but yes there is definitely love hidden somewhere. Love with a spirituality for mankind, though it's much on the ebbing end these days.

The more you think, the more you get overwhelmed by the depth of this four letter word. Its essence lies in its purity but 'life' is not a four letter word like 'love'. Its innuendoes are many and so it corrupts, by putting question marks, by submerging it's halo with a mist, by making one feel ashamed at times for harbouring it, makes and mars to an extent unimaginable. Sad indeed! Blessed is that one in a thousand who can proudly say "Yes, I have been loved for myself, yes, I have had the feel of what it is to be loved, in the true sense of the word."

Oh! To be able to feel its dewy purity in the pores of one's being.

34: ASPECT of LIFE***HEAR ME OUT

"Hear me out" and sure enough you'll have a queue waiting to do so. Friends and relatives, perhaps more sympathetic shoulders to lean on, you may never come across. Soon your confidences will be found making a 'merry go round' in their circles, while you find yourself stripped of all your vestige of respect. The councillor, who will sit across the table, nodding his/her head in apparent sympathy, corroding your stomach with asked for or un-asked for questions and then like a nerdy will rattle off a list of do's and don'ts, for your eternal bliss. All this not out of any empathy but simply because he/she is getting paid for the trained job, excellently done away with. The colleagues who will in no time, turn your 'heart-baring' to their advantage, making you appear, no less than a fool in your own eyes.

How many are there who will "hear you out" in the true sense of the term? Not even a handful. It's when you get the satisfaction of having been listened to, with an understanding, an empathy, with that connect, can you get the real feel of having 'been heard out'.

Recently I fleetingly met a lady who was in deep trouble with her husband and she would cry her heart out to me, while I'd 'hear her out' by way of all that it connotes. After her leaving, we both maintained our contact. A couple of days back I got a text from her "I want to talk to you". Immediately my problems took a back seat as I called her up. What did I do for her? I simply listened to her, while I made myself 'stand in her shoes'. As she cried through miles across, I could feel the tears stinging my eyes. It's the vibes which can carry across oceans. After a while I got another text from her "You can't understand how my talking to you has helped me out. Thanks so much".

Just that little time dedicated only to her . . . as I 'heard her out' . . . as though her woes were mine . . . a small act of kindness . . . which costs nothing . . . but can add milestones to one's life.

35: ME***DECISIONS

"When you are drowning, you learn to swim." Very true and this stands as a gaping truth, well nigh honoured by me. My period of vacillating like a pendulum from one end to the other, is pretty short lived and it's during this vacillation that I come to grips and make a decision. The latter is always a dicey proposition, for at that juncture you are like staring at a 'gaping-hole' in which you may fall or safely pass by. Nevertheless once that barrier is crossed, I'm prepared to deal with the consequences, for the better or the worse.

As I stand before the chasm my gut-instinct plays a major role and then as though out of the blue, something hits me and my decision is made. It's rarely that I revert on what I have decided upon, unless of course my heart melts, the emotional fool that I am. My made-up mind takes a U turn only regarding inter-personal relationships and that too when I start feeling strongly about my having hurt someone's feelings and not because my decision has not had enough reasons to support it. This too, when all the good done for me by that person keeps giving me its winsome smile. My pragmatism gets swallowed by emotional logistics.

I remember the time, when as a child I was, as usual running after a butterfly to catch it. It so happened a thorn from the rose bush pricked my finger and I ran howling and shrieking to my father and almost pulled the roof down, while the thorn was being removed. This was me and today I stand an entirely different person . . . who has learnt the hard way to grapple with life . . . but has kept that dew like purity well within her . . . that child in her even now peeps from corners . . . as she decides . . . as she allows the goodness of others to nullify her decision.

36: ME***"HAPPY B'DAY"

"Happy B'day to you, happy B'day to you . . ." and me standing, dressed up like a fairy, with that beaming smile on my face, as I bend to cut the B'day cake on a laced doily, ordered from the Moses Confectioners and then the clapping and the merriment as do I blow out candles, one after another. The games and the delicacies with me having my way, the more, that day because it happened to be my B'day and then when all was quiet, throwing a tantrum "Papa why can't I have my B'day every day?" Of course no amount of reasoning or cajoling would help pacify that B'day girl.

Today, on my B'day, the 13th of May, that impish B'day girl is a mature, middle-aged lady, who can look back and still smile that endearing smile with a wink, or who can look ahead with a wisdom and an understanding smile with as naughty a wink. Years have been lived by, existed by or learnt by, as though so many lives have been compressed into one whole. An ongoing process of learning and growth. It's been a tough journey of sorts, a sojourn which could have either mentally crippled me, or simply made me throw up my hands in dismay. I permitted neither, as I battled on, following the voice of my conscience, my guiding force. Little did I fathom or even thought of the outcome of it all or what remained at the end of the dark tunnel.

Today after having traversed a large part of the tunnel, I can see that light at the other end, a light ever so bright and clear, as though moving so fast towards me. All the darkness seems to be submerged with that beatific glaze, as does it bathe me with its sparkling feel. An evolvement of myself, bordering on the spiritual, a feeling of warmth and humanity towards the less privileged, a sense of pity for those who are so deep-neck-down with the flimsy side of life and an ensuing calm and peace as do I look back. Nothing can break me now, so sure am I of myself and the ground on which I stand, as of now and always will.

That sweet, spoilt, little fairy, in her fairy-land of B'days, ventures to celebrate each day as her B'day now. Not with a cake ordered from Moses but with the pruning of her lackings, as she does steadfastly move on towards the end of the tunnel, leaving the shreds behind, for she knows, the real B'day cake still awaits her, with it's candles innumerable.

37: ME***HAPPY MOTHER'S DAY

Happy Mother's Day to you my dearest Mummy. I know you to be in Heaven with Papa, since you left me ever so suddenly on that unforgettable evening of the 6th of November 2011. Though I was broken hearted and didn't know which way to look, it all seemed so blank, yet did I feel all the time, of your happiness at being with Papa after having lived without him for 22 long years. With what grace, dignity, strength, as loving and caring towards everyone as was Papa, did you live by yourself, Mama, you who had been kept so lovingly and protected by Papa.

Mummy it's been almost two years now without your being around, still not a day has gone by without you and Papa in my thoughts. As many a times do my tears dry up on my lashes and my sobs get stifled in my throat. My heart aches to go to Lucknow but somewhere deep down my steps stall, for everything though remains the same, still nothing is the same. The excitement a couple of stations before seeing the huge signboard 'Lucknow Station', running from inside the gate to fling myself like a free bird into your welcoming, open arms, the memories make my heart so heavy, as I lower myself on to the platform now. The few times when I have gone after you went, though everything is as you had left still do I move around like a robot, touching your pillow, feeling the warmth of your clothes in the almirahs, looking at yours and Papa's wedding photograph on the mantelpiece, as my cold fingers feel the contours, with a nostalgia so intense.

"Bindiya, it's been 4 months now and you haven't come to Lucknow". Remember for you and Papa I was never Vandana but always "Bindiya". It's close to 7 months since I went to Lucknow last and my ears ache to hear that sentence once again, my ears ache to hear someone calling me "Bindiya" but all that meets my ears is that dreadful silence. I realised that moment you left me, how a huge chapter of my life, brimming over with undefined love and care, had closed down forever. At least after Papa went, you were there, beautifully taking his place as well but after you none.

Mummy, you and Papa, though not physically present, are there beside me, every minute because I breathe, I think and behave in the manner you would have liked me to. Will I not till my last breath, be a part of you and Papa? Though I do stand today as an entity of my own but will ever remain your "sweet, naughty, little Bindiya" doing you proud at every step . . . (This is my tribute to you, Mummy, Mama, Mumsy and Amma on this Mother's day. A Mummy who is forever.)

38: ASPECT of LIFE***
CHARITY BEGINS AT HOME?

One of the proverbs which I find most grounded and applicable to our day to day lives is "Charity begins at home." It's much akin to your taking the first step regarding anything because if things go wrong at the grass root level the entire balance is going to tilt.

This adage appears so simple when heard, yet is it so difficult when put into practice. Let me start with myself. If I don't love myself will I be able to love others? If I can't respect myself will I be able to respect others? If I can't be happy will I be able to keep others happy? If I can't be at peace will I be able to keep others peaceful? If I can't look after the members of my family or my helps how can I look after those who are outside?

It's all there within me and it's for me to open the doors for the sunshine to seep in and from here will start my footsteps However with most of the people these days the proverb goes thus "Charity begins outside". Why do I write this with such conviction? I have observed many for whom nothing matters at home, so swallowed up are they with their wrong priorities. A more 'my dear crony' can never be, though a scowling husband at home. One who knows jolly well how to respect outsiders but showing an iota of respect to his wife is like a challenge to his manhood. Always around to lend a helping hand to those who simply have to mention so, though his wife maybe crying nights out due to the pain in her joints. I call such apologies of charity 'the pseudo Messiahs'.

Likewise the women also, will do anything to gain the love and respect from the world outside their home, spending hours for the benefits of their breed, with hardly any energy left for their family and household. It can go to the dogs for all they care, so long their plastic smiles are making their media rounds. The modus operandi of such men and women is much the same.

Little do these pseudoites realise how fruitless their endeavours are. This momentary satisfaction is ever so transient, providing a hollow, false sense of well being. All the pats on the back, the lunches and dinners, the video cams flashing in the face capturing that wide, satisfying smile, the sycophancy, the doling out of bundles of notes for social causes, of course to make a front page column in the newspapers the next day, for what?

Deep down do you know whether your charity has won you laurels or deprived you of your own real self? For you knew not how to love yourself, for you knew not how to respect yourself, for you knew not what it was like to be happy and peaceful, for you knew not how to revere the limitless beauty which lies within the precincts of your home? That valuable time was frittered away in the endeavour to haplessly earn that public halo round your empty head, as do you stand naked in front of your own eyes, unloved, with no self-respect worth the name, unhappy and alone, for you were flying in the 'Seventh Heaven' when it was time to go full throttle with "Charity begins at home."

39: ASPECT of LIFE***MEN

Though being a woman, I have many a time tried to view things from a man's emotional point of view and have always found my heart heavy afterwards because a man does find himself so tied down with his emotions and feelings as compared to a woman.

It's not that men are deprived of a heart with it's resulting beats but are unable to express themselves as expressively as a woman does. How many men have I seen crying, even when in the throes of an immense personal tragedy? Yes, a short outburst of tears lasting barely a minute and then that extreme control over themselves. Are their attachments any less or their feelings any less? No they are as much as a woman undergoing the same pain of a memorable loss but while she gives vent to her feelings without the slightest reserve, men have all their reserves. It's no hidden fact, tears help largely to ease any grief and men but store it away in their hearts.

Many and believe me many men are, dominated by their wives but will seldom make it known in public, the main reason being the shame of being categorised as hen-pecked. With their mouths shut do they keep tolerating their wives overbearing skills behind closed doors desperately making a facade in front of others? I can well make myself stand in their shoes and get a harrowing feel of their resulting frustration and helplessness. While a woman at the slightest pretext will go around yapping her woes, imaginary or otherwise. Once again any means of a catharsis for men gets jeopardised.

Organisations for the protection, upliftment, safeguards of the so-called rights of women, are growing like mushrooms, hither and thither. What about men who go into deep debts, simply because their stupid wives know not how to live gracefully within their means? What about the lot who work hard, day in and day out, for their families but to see their hard earned money lost in gambling by those empty heads at the card tables? What about those men who see their wives flirting outrageously with other men at parties in front of their eyes but quietly look the other way because it's a splurge on their manliness? What about those men whose hearts cry in abject loneliness but deprive themselves from seeking a shoulder to cry upon because they will be labelled as effeminate? I say are there any organisations for helping men, caught in the web of their dismal misery? None so far to my knowledge?

Great! As always the women steal the show, by hook or by crook. Paint the men black but kiss their ass to get their end, and then once again kick them in the ass and walk towards the ever open doors of a woman's organisation, with the paparazzi in tow. A great deal splashed in the media for the derogatory treatment meted out to her, handkerchiefs getting wet by the dozen, as tears run oceans for the media darling, in media interviews. The man standing alone, with none to lend him an ear, even if he shouts himself hoarse. Eventually he finds himself put at par with no better a thing than a rotten egg, as he drags his legs towards a pub, with his tears locked up in his eyes, his respect sold for a lark, his emotions in tatters, and a big hole in his pocket, as the bartender pours out drink after drink, till he finds himself sozzled enough to lose himself in the intoxicating vapours, at least for the time being. My heart goes out for you men in all sincerity. Draw solace, at least there is one such a lady who has ventured to stand in your shoes and feel and emote the way you men do.

40: ME***THOSE SMALL SENTENCES

Nothing was imparted to me on a platter. It's just that every drop kept falling in place, finding it's right place and moving on with the flow, forming one consecutive whole. By this I refer to the many lessons one learns during those crucial, growing up years at home. It's all of these pearly drops, which eventually form the bed on which flows the river of life. Ever so undulating, rising and falling with the tide, sometimes coming to rest like the backwash but never still, always on the move.

These small sentences, made ever so substantial by their words, kept falling in my ears, whenever my parents thought it necessary to do so. "Never make a sound with the cutlery while eating. Never hold the fork in your right hand. When munching, not a sound should be there. You are not supposed to talk with a mouthful. Don't rest your elbows on the dining table. Always tilt the soup bowl in the opposite direction. Use the napkin like a lady. Start using the cutlery from outside in. When somebody wishes you with a 'How do you do?' you ought to reply with a 'How do you do?' with a slight change in the tone. Always sit with your legs together. Prying into anyone's diary is simply not done. Trying to overhear somebody's conversation is bad manners. Always reply to a letter received. Gaining or losing respect is in your own hands. Never show down a person. If your conscience tells you, what you are doing is right, do it because there is no voice higher than your own conscience. Respect your elders but the elders should also be worthy of that respect. When you start talking money, that money has lost it's worth. Never return a person empty handed, who has come to your doorstep with some hope. Before you become judgemental put your self in that person's shoes. Compromising on your values is a sign of weakness. Your end is as important as the means by which you achieve that end."

I can go on and on, as many more inadvertently kept making their silent way into my system, becoming so much a part and parcel of my being, my backbone of life. Small nothing's, so did they seem at that point of time yet the stringent guidelines for my life ahead. I never have to look here and there, when finding myself in a fix, for the answer is always there within me, I need just to turn a few pages, to grapple with those small sentences, on which flows the river of my life.

41: ASPECT of LIFE***QUIET MOORINGS

Have you ever sat back quietly, losing yourself to the innumerable touches which have left their soothing mark or a dent in your life? Maybe if you try to recall you won't even be able to pick out the figure from the hazy silhouettes before you. Yet each step that has stepped into your life, has left its footprint, for the better or the worse. As do they uplift or submerge your emotions, as do they make your faltering footsteps firmer or weaker, as do they cement or disillusion your view of life. Many maybe the footsteps which have silently gone out of your life forever, never to return but have left indelible marks all around, to be cherished or trampled upon but can they be ever erased?

The flora and fauna likewise join hands in skipping through your days. That blooming red rose, smiles it's warm passionate smile, a remembrance of your first love, as it awakened vistas of those euphoric feelings, hitherto unknown. Those white orchids, decorated so elegantly in a florist's shop, peeping from the window, waters your eyes as you are reminded of the bouquet of white orchids, laid at your friend's funeral, a friend who always did do justice to her being called a friend. Those pink lotus, so virgin, floating above the muddy water, untouched.

The birds, bees and the butterflies, with their cacophony or fluttering of wings, as though resonating nature's charms. Each one of them, ever so busy with their Herculean tasks, carrying them out with that single-mindedness, so lacking in we humans. None trespassing on the other's limits, no heartburns, no expectations. The birds merrily chirping away, rocking on the branches of the trees, after a hard day's work. The busy bees, as they buzz in and out of their bee-hives, having stacked their home enough with honey, after a hard day's toil. The butterflies, gaily hopping from one flower to another, getting drunk on the intoxicating sweetness of the nectar. All reminders in their own subtle manner of how life can be handled, if only certain primitive laws of nature are adhered to.

No amount of literacy can impart the education which one can amass from witnessing these small mysteries of life around. So open yet so closed.

Always there, willingly reaching out, it's only for you to understand and allow the feel to remain. As do they always do, though you may not feel them so but somewhere deep down these riddles are at work, for the better or the worse, depending on how you allow them to reach out to you. Those footsteps with their quiet moorings.

42: ASPECT of LIFE***WALL

Those 'walls' which can come up in any relationship. It's only a matter of the first brick to make its way to the foundation, the rest of the bricks quickly start making their way too in no time. Soon the 'wall' starts to gain height and rapidly becomes so high, as to make it impossible to climb across.

Have you ever tried to take time out and give a thought, to a relationship which has gone haywire? Hardly ever because you become such an easy prey to the 'blame-game', as garbage and muck is liberally thrown at each other. Easiest remedy to absolve yourself from taking the onus, at least that little bit. You can never clap with one hand but no here, from both the ends, the clapping has been done, with just one hand. The other hand has been simply listening to the 'melody of the clapping.' It's sad indeed, to see any relationship slowly but steadily giving way. You permit the first brick to make a stronghold, a base, not making the slightest bit of effort the kick it off, in one go.

That false ego, bloated sense of self-importance, the 'me' so paramount, no time to sit and introspect and retrospect because there are other important things to be taken care of. Stealthily but surely, one brick finds its way on the other and the bricks start getting cemented, as the 'wall' starts to get higher. Each standing helplessly on either side of the 'wall', the 'wall' risen so high as to make it impossible to look at the other side, what talk of climbing, the hands which clasped each others, the understanding that was, that sweet little world of happiness and sorrows shared, all but gone asunder. Simply because none paid any attention, when the first brick of the 'wall' took its first step.

43: ASPECT of LIFE***
DATES IN THE CALENDAR

'Those dates in the calendar', with what exuberance and utter delight their arrival was awaited from the beginning of the year, the elders sharing the excitement as much, if not more. The visits to the tailor, the selection of the designs for the frocks from the catalogue, to be subsequently embroidered with a few carnations by Mummy, here and there. The aroma of the delicacies wafting through the house, from days ahead and then finally the much awaited day at the doorstep. 'Holi' and the shouts and the laughter as we ran around with the colours, the guffaws and the clapping, as someone was literally picked up and dipped in a drum of water mixed with colour. The merging colours, so far gone, as to make it difficult for us to decipher one from the other, followed by the Herculean task of cleaning it away, with an equal amount of merriment. Thereafter getting all dolled up for the guests and the visits, the delicacies served and offered with as much warmth and hospitality.

Where is it all gone, everywhere? Have we so far distanced ourselves from those small human touches, which form the base of a joyous life? Where has vanished that gusto and buoyancy which beckoned the arrival of that 'date in the calendar'? The little that remains is merely a skeleton of the memories of what was. It's only the working class which celebrates all the festivals with as much zest and vigour, despite their day to day hassles and financial limitations. Being a witness to their never ending enthusiasm, have I realised that it's all in the mind.

What matters is the desire automatically getting clubbed with the spirit and the zeal, which they have still been able to retain. Whereas we have been a lot blessed, still there is a huge hollowness around, simply because we have lost touch with those small, little joys of life, which makes life so complete. 'The dates in the calendar' are merely dates now, to be rolled away in the calendar, at the end of the year and thrown away.

44: ASPECT of LIFE***LAW OF THE JUNGLE

Population explosion, rising aspirations in the people of all classes, the frantic compulsion to amass as much wealth and material benefits at a nerve breaking speed, twenty-four hours of the day falling as though short, women parading the streets with "We are proud to be a woman". What is the end result going to be?

Total chaos in every sphere of life, with commotion at its best. When everything starts vying for equality then either there will be an all pervading peace or the whole system gets tilted, with everyone having a ball. Corruption becomes rampant starting from the lowest rung of the ladder and swiftly climbing to the highest. A 'home' ceases to exist, the walls falling apart with the seeming sense of equality, and over-taxed bodies. Divorces and the worse hit are the children, who find other means to fulfil that parental-care void in their lives. People willing to sacrifice everything at the altar, their values, self-respect, every bit that goes into building that sense of human dignity, in quest of their ambition. Facade and duplicity becomes the order of the day, with one not knowing when a seeming friend takes the place of an enemy. A thumping rise in the crime rate, what with the safeguards of society themselves heaving under this uncontrollable scenario, the cheapest commodity in the market, being the life of a human being.

They were not fools who laid down the norms of leading a balanced life, eventually laying the base for a healthy society. Every bit has tampered with the laws, leading to a sick society made up of sucked out people, squeezed out of even that minimum worth which makes a human being stand apart. The 'law of the jungle' prevails, wherein each and everyone lives by his or her own norms, wherein each is at the mercy of the other, a vicious never ending circle of mayhem.

45: ASPECT of LIFE***DOG HEAVEN

Dogs are always associated with whatever, in a derogatory manner... 'Let the barking dogs bark'... 'Men are dogs'... and so on so forth. Still unaware of the humiliating innuendoes they continue to be what their good sense demands of them, far superseding us with their unconditional goodness.

Ever steadfastly loyal to their master, more than happy with whatever little or much comes their way. A devotion unparalleled, ready to attack at the slightest bit of animosity shown towards their master, guarding him like a guardian angel, round the clock and not only him but all the members of his family. Lo and behold, if a stranger happens to walk in and the dog is not on a leash, well then the person has no other option but to throw up his hands. It's bewildering how their senses are so sharp. The car turns at the corner and their squealing to be pampered, meets your ears. Any morbid happening and their howling, prophecies so much in advance. The sniffer dogs unearthing clues beyond the efforts of we humans. A child will take months to get trained but with them it's a matter of days.

What more, a widow will stick to the minimum days of mourning, before her eyes start to hunt for another groom, whereas the master's dog's faithfulness continues, undeterred, as he goes and sleeps on the grave protecting his master even when he is no more. A devotion and loyalty unparalleled, no minus points in merits, as compared to many with we humans, hence there is always a 'Dog Heaven' never a 'Dog Hell'.

46: ASPECT of LIFE***NOVEL

Every person's life is indeed a novel, it simply remains for one to view it with this perspective. At the moment of conception, the pages start to turn, unravelling the text, with each day as it goes by. A beginning and an end, with chapters innumerable, spelling out the happenings, the circumstances which led to those happenings and vice-versa . . . justifying or not the person's handling of those small touches which make their presence felt at every step . . . the lessons learnt or let go by . . . the personal evolvement depending so much on the manner in which things are perceived and turned to one's advantage or permitted to override and have their way. A novel whose pages throb with the intermingling of the lives of characters innumerable, the interesting intersections by way of each other's moments of happiness and sorrow. Gradually the dwindling of the characters as some leave forever, some who come like a whiff of fresh breeze and then disappear as quickly with their soothing touches, the many who keep by your side through thick and thin and those who leave by way of no explanation. Each interlude to be remembered and jotted down because none come and go without a purpose.

Illustrations so many, by way of memories etched in the mind. One simply has to draw aside the curtain and the scenes stand before the eyes, as though yesterday, the years wiped away in the blink of an eye. Emoting, the emotions taking a grip as everything starts to turn pages, as though the pictures of a novel. Biographies are penned, autobiographies are penned, selling for a price, because they spell out the life of celebrities. None bother to peep into the lives of so many, many whose pages can stand as a testimony of life, giving a flavour, lending a hand, to all those who need a light in the plunging darkness and let their lightened paths, become a succour of hope for others because every person's life is a 'novel'.

47: ASPECT of LIFE***THE COMMON MAN

The middle-class or the common man sandwiched betwixt the prosperous and the poor . . . the worse hit . . . not only by way of the norms laid down by society . . . not only by way of financial constraints . . . but most by the day-to-day difficulties faced at every step . . . endless steps in the journey of life. For them to make meet their simple and basic needs on a shoe-string budget, is like trying to make the sky and the earth meet. Follows a rapid round of loans and borrowing, with the rest of the life spent in scavenging to pay back the debts, what talk of the expenses to be met on a day-to-day basis? Everyday waking up to the call of the rising sun, and somehow creeping into bed with a body devoid of all energy, after a day spent in commuting by public transport, standing with tired legs in endless quest, trying desperately to hide the holes in the worn-out clothing, shoes which refuse to hold together anymore, the changing climates are not for them to bother about as the feet move on relentlessly in the scorching sun or the biting cold.

Who doesn't wish to care for the small needs of the family? Which parents are dead to the wanting cries of their children? Eyes which look up with a longing, never to be fulfilled, at the maze of upcoming apartments . . . weary legs which shuffle past the five star hotels, where the guard at the gate will bar entry . . . standing in the buses, watching the expensive cars whizzing past . . . empty pockets, which throw all dreams to the winds.

Still sometimes smiling, sometimes crying, at their fate, at the wantings of a common man . . . still every breath has to be lived by . . . a respite from the travails only to come by, when the body which can hold no more, bids it's final adieu.

48: ASPECT of LIFE***JUSTICE

Why do we harp on 'justice'? The 'justice' for which we depend upon on the courts of law. A 'justice' which many never remain to see, a 'justice' for which each breath for years had been begging for, like a lender begging for his own money.

Years burnt away with convicts, in the atrocious conditions of a jail, simply because of an F.I.R. filed in one's name, and the humiliation to be succumbed to, many a times for years, because of the tardiness of our judicial process. The third degree punishment meted out to a suspect, for divulging know-how's of a crime, a crime he has never committed and his silence registered as his consent to the commitment of the crime, enough of an excuse to further sharpen the methods for breaking a rightful silence. To enter the court room with hand-cuffs on and a sentry on either side, simply because one is in the list of suspects, and then to be hauled again amidst the physical and emotional filth, because the procedure of the court has to be looked into.

Thankfully when the court has gone through all the legalities, of course time goes endless, 'justice' is meted out. Will I call it 'justice'? Who will bring back those whose cries for 'justice' went unheard while alive? Who will erase those scars from the mind, scars which have no business to be there, simply because one was at the mercy of the legal process? Who will give back those seconds which got lost amidst the squalor and the humiliation? Nobody? The horrendous experiences to which the close ones were subjected to, never to be erased from memory. Who will compensate for their tragic days? Nobody. Still we harp on 'justice' depending for it on our courts of law, which are themselves crippled by the nuances of the legal process, the entire system based on 'evidence' real or planted and it becomes the platform for 'justice?'

49: ASPECT of LIFE***VENDETTA

When in my teens I had read the novel *Vendetta* and it had left a deep impact on my mind, an impact which has its grip over me, even today. A lesson learnt for eternity about vengeance. It's only a matter of the thought of seeking revenge to make its silent entry into your system and gradually it starts to loom like a horrific shadow in your life.

Not a minute's peace as you scheme and plot, day in and day out, in terms of hurting that person with a greater wound, than the one inflicted on you. Days become a 'board of chess', when and where to make the appropriate moves, as nights become a nightmare, a witness to the turbulence in the mind. It's as though you are intoxicated with the fumes of revenge.

A beautiful life gets tainted with the effects of hatred in the eyes, the eyes always directed towards the target. Finally when the fatal day arrives and all your energy gets focused on the victim, the vendetta for which you wasted this precious life plays its role. Silence awaits you, a deadly silence, in which you hear your conscience screaming for redemption, the frightening echoes come hitting back, as you cower, victorious or defeated, time alone will tell . . . (I remember a shiver running down my spine, as I had finished the book, and could get the feel of the same shiver as my fingers were moving on my iPad.)

50: ME***A HOMEMAKER

Invariably the query which comes up from a stranger, after meeting me for a while is "Are you working?" And each time have I, without a hitch and pride, replied, "Yes, I am working as a homemaker." Every time with a smile have I noticed that little look of surprise in the eyes which sets me wondering at many a fleeting thoughts which cross my mind.

Can a homemaker not be prettily smart, articulate, confident and qualified and if she happens to be thus, then well does she have to be a career woman? As though a homemaker goes around donning an apron to announce as much. Little is it realised how tough it is to be a homemaker and yet so fulfilling, a position with its own prerogatives. A round the clock honorary job, working selflessly to make a home within the precincts of a concrete house, a home which dwells amidst the laughter, happiness and the love of a husband and children, my love beaming through my eyes as I look upon. The time is always at my disposal, no hurry and scurry, as I pleasantly go around with my work, making time stand on its toes for me. To crush my individuality and keep mouthing 'Yes Boss' at being fired for the Boss's fault and to give that pleasing smile always, while cursing him under my breath, for fear of being thrown out, is decidedly not 'my cup of tea.' As my husband once told me, "You can't stick in a job for more than a week." Well that's putting it mildly, I give myself just a couple of days.

Can working as a career woman ever give me the quality of satisfaction which I get as a homemaker? No never because the day will go by working as a robot at the behest of someone else, whatever little time doled out to me for holding hands of love with my family, will be slotted for duties so many, so where will be the minutes to make a house throb with the bouncing love of a home? Whenever I so desire I stand before the mirror and pat my own back, when I need one such pat, as I hear the loving laughter as a backdrop and the biggest reward of me as homemaker falls into my lap on it's own . . . (I have used the word homemaker and not housewife because there lies a very fine difference betwixt the two, the same as what lies betwixt a Mommy and a Mummy.)

51: ASPECT of LIFE***PROSTITUTION

Prostitution, a word, a profession, to be sneered at, to be compartmentalised with what is illegal. Fine so far so good but what about the girls/women who sleep with their colleagues or bosses for professional gains, putting their self-respect at bay. Is this not prostitution? What about those wives who spend night or nights with their husband's boss, selling their loyalty simply to see their husband, a rung higher on that ladder of success? Is this not prostitution? The in-fashion wife-swapping, for the heck of it, or to satisfy their sexual craving. Is this not prostitution? No, this is not categorised as such. Why, because they don't live in brothels and are the so-called respected girls/women of society, who under the garb of respectability, bare themselves for gains varied. Why, because they don't stand on the pavements to lure men but do the same in a manner befitting their monetary worth. Why are there no police raids in their respectable houses because their nakedness is flaunted under the shrouds of privacy? The prostitutes and these girls/women, both sell themselves to men by way of sexual favours, for personal gains. The former do it for money to sustain themselves and the latter for material privileges. The prostitutes make no bones about their prostitution, at least they are honest, as compared to these 'so-called respected members of society' who cover their prostitution under the garb of respectability and status. Still the prostitutes are castigated in society for their honesty, still no 'stone is left unturned' to bring their nudity in full public glare, whereas these girls/women who are no better, go scot-free, because of their facade, because their dishonesty gets lost in the folds of their respectability.

52: ASPECT of LIFE***SO FAR GONE

We invite those for a meal who already have enough to eat. We make them happy with gifts whose houses are overflowing with material benefits. We never fail or take time out somehow, to make our presence felt, on their happy or solemn occasions. Why, because social obligations have to be come by with those who either fall into our family, friends, or official arena.

Fine in order to survive socially, these obligations have to be adhered to. However do we ever give a thought to those who as 'helps' around the house, give us all those comforts, which shows itself in every corner of the house, which quietly garnishes the dishes on the table, which sees to the call of our smallest need, feelings which get hurt at the rebukes, if the smallest duty has not been well looked into?

No, because they are getting paid for the hours that are being put into and have been bought due to their poverty. No matter what their problems, we never bother to help them out, because they were born to struggle, marriages or funerals in their families are not for us to consume our precious time with, left-overs at parties' falls into their lot, after their culinary skills have pleased our palates.

Have we so distanced ourselves from humane feelings as to have degraded ourselves by treating them as mere guinea pigs, bought for pittance, those who stand by us, when our own spouse or children don't have the time to even be around? Yes we have because we know not how to respect humanity . . . we know not, whether privileged or underprivileged, we are all born with the same feelings and emotions, all we know is about, whatever money or status, can give us or whatever we can stretch ourselves to do, as slaves of both.

53: ME***NEVER TOO LATE

Many, many years back, maybe soon after my wedding, we had some friends over for dinner and one of them happened to remark "I really don't know but I get a lot effected by the pain of others." That night as I was trying to sleep her sentence stood out quizzically against the darkness and set me thinking. "How is it possible to get effected by the pain of others?" It was beyond me to comprehend thus, since I was still living in that fairy-tale world of my pre-marriage days, though much on the outskirts by now.

Days and years went by, not a day the same, not a year like the one before, to have touched 2013 now. Today that sentence no longer stands out against the darkness, it stands as though against a blessed light, getting flooded by its soothing effect, a process of transformation. My heart bleeds when I see the trauma of the people around, I question myself "What am I doing to help?" I question God "If you are there, then why is there so much pain?" The answers I get, when I do whatever little I can by way of rendering those small human touches to those who never return from my threshold with a broken hope. The answer I get when I see someone crushed to the bones, getting compensated in a manner unthought of, by the will of God. My problems get diluted, appearing ever so small, before the unassailable problems of others, giving me the strength to 'reach out' by way of my little best, and fit in a small, small corner of 'God's manner of compensation.'

54: ASPECT of LIFE***
TO HELL WITH THE WORD AUNTY

What's there in the 'mode of addressing' a woman as 'Aunty'? Oh! Yes there's a lot, it's almost a matter of life and death for most. Women get wild enough to chew up that person alive, if they get offended with this word. Just call a woman 'Aunty' if you happen to be a little here and there, around her age? Suddenly without the least bit of intimation you'll hear an ear-banging voice "How dare you call me Aunty? Am I your Aunty or you mine?" or she'll get claws, as though ready to claw out your eyes, as you stand transfixed, gaping like a gold fish, wondering what went wrong where? Little do these gullible ones realise the volumes crushed in this small, little word.

A woman remains touchy about her age, even at the ebbing days of eighty long years, and addressing one as 'Aunty' brings this delicate age factor, as though hitting hard on the face. All decorum goes 'for a lark' as they throw all caution to the winds, fighting like 'cats and dogs' over this 'harmless' yet so 'harmful' a word. As though by not being addressed as 'Aunty' will bring back the lost youth and make her look ever 'sweet sixteen'.

55: ASPECT of LIFE***EACH DAY

No day is the same as the other, each dawn with its own story in tow. Everyone wakes up to the call of dawn, completely oblivious to what lies in store ahead. Some wake up with a 'song on the lips', and the passing day holds testimony, whether the song remains or is wafted away by the minutes. "Oh! Another day like all other days, nothing ever happening to break the monotony" and as though suddenly out of the blue comes happiness in some form or the other and the heart begins to sing. Most of the days are placed like any other day and slide by becoming one more in the hues of the past.

How helpless are we, as though waiting for the minutes to unfold and bring forth whatever lies in store for the better or the worse. Most endeavour to do the best they can by way of letting the smile remain on the lips but humans will remain humans, and many a happenings sap the endurance at some point or the other. Still we continue to wait for the rising sun to cover each day like a soft blanket with it's sunny rays, and cuddle into our bed under the soft light of the moon, to wake up to the 'call of another day' unfolding it's mysteries with each breath, as it goes by.

56: ASPECT of LIFE***ANNIVERSARIES

We have 'anniversaries' for every important event in our lives, by way of commemorating that special event which had occurred on the same date of the previous years. For me any 'anniversary' is a day when I re-live that particular day which has made such an indelible mark on my life. That particular day which stands out amongst the rest of the 364 days of the year. Its laden with memories, and it's almost as though the curtain has been drawn away from those number of days and it stands out clearly before me with the person around whom the day revolved.

Introspection and retrospection of a magnitude of related events come rushing back, as they jostle my mind. So much is accepted and a lot is filtered as I educate myself with the legacies of learning left behind. A bundle of emotions do I become, as my feelings get the better of me. A craving to be with that missing person once again, that memorable day of my marriage, till today, an on-going process of learning, with a catch in the throat here and smile there do I sit lost, as the past takes hold over the present, and the present moves into the future, with a wiser me, looking ahead, towards another year, with one more year added to that 'anniversary.'

57: ASPECT of LIFE***TREES

Ever seen a grove of trees? Each tree standing by itself, so alone and yet so together, giving the feel of their utter independence by way of managing themselves and yet being by each other, come hail, come storm. They don't demand any care, drawing their nutrition from the earth, and yet giving forth as much as they can, unasked for and demanding nothing in return. At the 'beck and call' of the seasons, do they flower into fruits, apples laden there, apricots so smiling in the branches, mangoes by the dozen. Name any fruit and the giver are of course the trees. The enamouring foliage covered with the sprinkling of flowers seem to depict the various hues of life. Their greenery exuding so much positivity that it sends many a hearts singing. Tired travellers take a breather under its welcoming, cool, breezy shade, as the branches spread their arms to give them succour. Seeming to talk endless in their whisperings, with the breeze blowing, the kernels resounding the sound of the merriment. At night their silhouettes against the sky, with the glory of the moon and the twinkling stars, holds one spellbound, by their mystique beauty. A source of sustenance for so many, every part of theirs yielding some benefit or the other, they sure are a haven for so many. Given the chance I'd much rather befriend them because they can always be depended upon and they are so much their own, natural selves.

58: ASPECT of LIFE***OLD AGE

Old age is perhaps the saddest and the most disillusioning phase of one's life. The person around whom lives and activities revolved, suddenly finds himself or herself alone with only memories to give company, bringing a smile here and a sob there. It must be so horrifying to feel the emptiness around, groping in the dark for a hand to give support, expectantly listening in the deadening quietude for the chattering with the intermittent laughter, craving for the warmth of arms around hugging the solitary shoulders but all that meets is the deadening silence. I can feel the wrenching of the heart, the helplessness and the feeling of utter desolation.

To think of those days when nothing moved without that presence, so many lives dependent, the thread which tied all into one, always there tending to the needs and calls of so many. Now when every minute of the days look with that childish expectation for the presence of just one, from the many that were, there is no hope of even one, bending over with that same love and concern, which was there never for asking because it was understood and felt and given.

All have flown away and made their nests, tied down with their own lives, where to think and spare a couple of days for those lonely breaths, becomes a Herculean task, for aren't there much more important things to be taken care of? The lonely figure so alone, never once grudges, never once complains, the tears and smiles hidden in the depths, trying to hear the coming footsteps, the voices and the giggles, the loving arms around . . . to soothe away the loneliness.

59: ASPECT of LIFE***NO VALUE FOR VALUES

'Value for values' has decidedly gone to
the dogs. Its perhaps only 'stupid people' like me who hold onto our value
system. On the general plane, living by values is murder of the material
benefits, by which a person's worth is measured in inches today.

"Why live by the values of yore, when it's a minus zero gain?" Do
whatever enters your head, lie, murder, commit adultery, embezzle or
whatever, to meet your material ends, is the bizarre line of thought. Of
course relationships don't matter or matter as little and why will they, when
all that you see, hear or speak is money and money and money. Cheat on
whoever you can, your parents, siblings, friends to get those material
benefits, which are a measure of your social status. Little do these buffoons
fathom the triviality of such 'material gains' because all that they can see are
the so-called gains, they have surrounded themselves with and not the 'real
loss' they have incurred in the process.

Gone to the winds are the character benefits, gone to the winds are
those cherished ties of a relationship, and above all, gone to the winds is that
respect for your own self. Shying to meet your own eyes in your reflection, is
what you have gained or lost by living a life, where 'values have gone to the
dogs.'

60: ASPECT of LIFE***
PASSION, AN ESCAPE ROUTE

Why do you immerse yourself in whatever be your passion in life? Why is it you anyhow find the time for it, sometimes at the cost of a few sundry things here and there? Ever tried to pragmatically analyse it?

I have, to the realisation that in many ways its simply an 'escape route' from whatever be that 'looming problem' in your life. It may be your memories, a family problem, a work-place deficit, a betrayal or whatever, since there can never be an end to problems in life. It's just that there is always one such which un-wantingly makes its presence felt over everything else. There are those very few who are able to balance it out, the rest while doing their best by way of handling it, eventually find a means, to delve in, thereby switching their minds off from the engulfing fog. You get lost to everything else around, as you lose yourself into the depths of your passion, to the beauty of your passion, to the hidden mysteries of your passion, finding in it a 'means of escape' from that 'looming problem'.

61: ASPECT of LIFE***FORGIVE AND FORGET

These words have come down the ages . . . 'forgive and forget'. It's easier said than done. Forgiving fine but forgetting is decidedly not easy. The question which rattles my mind is, how can I forgive when I have been unable to forget? Unable to forget the hurt which in my quiet moments never fails to bring tears in my eyes. Unable to forget the humiliation undergone, still corroding the inners. Unable to forget my innocence pitted against the craftiness of many and the trials gone through therewith.

I am sure all humans are endowed with the power of memory and the memory registers it all, coming from the subconscious to the conscious at the convenience of the circumstances. Is it humanly possible to erase unwanted memories? Yes perhaps then it will be possible to forgive at the moment, of the wrong done, because with the mind sans the happening later, where is the chance for any hurt to remain? This is as impossible as expecting the sun to rise at night and the moon during the day.

I have pondered a great deal on this 'forgive and forget' aspect but each time have I been compelled to the conclusion, that 'forgiveness' is merely mouthed because an act which calls for 'forgiveness' can never be 'forgotten'. Yes time can, to a large extent, minimise the intensity of the rancour but can never make the mind a clean slate, so as to really be able to 'forgive' with the full conviction of 'forgiveness'.

62: ASPECT of LIFE***EXCUSES

Making excuses is the easiest thing to do, in order to save one's skin. Many may argue "I make an excuse so as not to hurt a person" . . . another will put forth the defence "I do so to avoid an unpleasant situation" and so on so forth. Excuses for making excuses go endless.

Little is it fathomed that excuses fall flatly in the category of lies and one lie leads mercilessly to another in a mounting frenzy of self-defence. It's not as though one doesn't realise that an excuse has been made, making the person fall in the eyes, unless of course both take recourse to excuses. Well then it hardly matters, it's then tit for tat. Why uselessly waste your energy on cooking up an excuse and then keep draining out further energy to keep the excuse intact.

I for one can never indulge in this fake art and politely refuse (if the need be) giving forth my genuine reasons for the refusal, of whatever it be. My conscience is at rest and at the same time I'm spared the hassle of building a mountain of lies due to one stupid excuse because I didn't have the courage to speak the truth, or simply because I didn't have the heart to hurt someone, little realising it's you who is the person hurt. What difference does it make to anyone else really?

63: ASPECT of LIFE***JOINT FAMILY

I have had the privilege of growing up in a joint family, which comprised of six uncles, my aunts and twenty-two cousins. Never knew when the day started and when the moon peeped from the sky. Playing endless and studying in whatever meagre time could be squeezed out was the order of the day, fun and frolic all the way, so beautifully balanced. Plays were organised and of course I would play the central character's role. A make-shift stage with a curtain would be set up in the garden and the audience would be the common relatives around, giving us a great projection.

Except for the personal rooms everything in the house was everyone's, thereby inculcating in us the qualities of sharing and giving. The parents seldom knew who was parenting whom, as long as we showed our faces now and then, inadvertently widened our horizons. Opening our hearts out to cousins closest to one's age or doing shared studies took care of our emotional and academic demands. Fighting mostly verbally like Hell, as and when, taught us to stand for our rights and budding views. Since my family was never bound down by religious rituals, my fourth aunt down the line would tell us stories from the Hindu mythology, keeping us in awe of the innumerable Gods and Goddesses, as we helped her in making the lemon and red chilly pickles in the garden.

Days bubbling by, packed to the brim with happiness hand in hand with fun and learning, moulding our characters with its feathery touches, a fairy-tale that set the ball rolling for the future to be handled to the best of our ability.

64: ASPECT of LIFE***THE BUTLER

Now the 'butlers' sure do take a grip over my imagination, always bringing to mind the 'stiff upper-lipped Jeeves, the butler', the central character of P.G. Wodehouse novels. Jeeves remarkably portrays a butler's true characteristics. They are a class by themselves being a predominant part of any affluent household, head of the male staff and in charge of the dining room, the pantry and the cellars. This is the official arena of a 'butler'.

The enamouring aspect, perhaps more predominant, is as stiffly hidden under their livery. Being such an integral part of the household, their reaches are far and beyond. The members will be oblivious to many a happenings within the precincts of the wall but not the 'butler'. Their main grapevine being their own ears jammed against the key-hole, keeping their faces straight despite their tummies churning with all the gossip inside. Must be quite an effort. It is his prerogative to hold the coat for the master of the house to wear, after the coat has been handed over to him by the footman. His affinity to the master of the house stands unquestioned.

It surely must be taking a lot to don a butler's black tail-coat, waist-coat, trousers and bow, to maintain the necessary demeanour with everyone around, knowing the best and worst of each, the irrepressible urge to spill the beans but then the job will be at stake, so it's best to be like the 'stiff upper-lipped Jeeves'.

65: ASPECT of LIFE***DIFFERENT

We are all so different and if not so life would perhaps become too mundane. Rightly has it been said "Variety is the spice of life." Leave alone others, all of us go through a process of change during the span of life.

I can talk for myself, I'm certainly not what I was down the lane. In fact when I take a peep I am amazed at myself, am I really the same person, I was thirty-five years back or am I a different person? It's as though I have been on a roller coaster ride but a real bumpy one. The bumps have hurt and made me wince at times, making me evolve, educating me about the crevices of life. The innumerable people I have willingly or unwillingly interacted with, too have rubbed me the right or the wrong way, lending that extra bit always for the better. Why do I say 'for the better'? I inadvertently started to sieve and allowed myself to imbibe whatever could be, to make myself a better me. Never did I allow myself to succumb or should I put it this way "A drowning person learns to swim."

Characters of people differ and they handle life accordingly, there are those who get embittered, there are those who throw their hands up, there are those to whom life has been kind and they carry on for the better or for the worse, and there are those like me who learn the art of facing life with equilibrium. Doesn't matter if a furrow has come betwixt my eyebrows, at least my eyes can still twinkle with that naughty gleam, nothing on earth can take away this gleam.

66: ME***ANGELS

I am often forced to wonder at human relationships, with those we grow up with . . . with those we cultivate, with those we just happen to come across. Each is blessed with its own landscaping, of give and take, of happiness and sorrow, of education and experiences.

However it's the 'connect' with those I haven't known since Adam which touches me to the core of my heart and reinstates my failing belief in the character syndrome of the people around. What is the need for a stranger or maybe someone I have barely known for some flying days to go out of his or her way to be kind to me by way of innumerable ways? There are barely any moments spent together and still there flows a rapport, a sharing of those moments of life so special, an unspoken understanding of each other's needs, helping in whatever way be feasible, is what makes me rekindle my hopes that there are still good people around.

We are under no obligation whatsoever, still that 'human connect' is so overpowering, so poignant as to belittle all other 'connects' which in some manner or the other rest heavily on the 'give and take platform' except of course that of the parents with their children. I thank my stars for being blessed enough to have had a flow of those, who when they stepped in were like a shadow from nowhere, and have now become an integral part of my life, making me a benefactor of that consoling thought, that yes there are still 'angels' around.

67: ASPECT of LIFE***EMPATHY

It's when tears roll down your cheeks, listening to the sorrow of someone you hardly know, then that is empathy. Today as I got talking to a bell boy, I seemed to have lost track of time, as he started relating the hardships that life had dealt out to him, but each time as though some miracle had come by. He almost lost his wife, the doctors having given up hope, but she did survive and is doing fine. His salary hardly enough to sustain his family, still he takes out whatever time and money he can to do charity. His contention being that by simply talking he can't repay for the blessings received, he has to prove his gratefulness by helping those in need. With Christmas just round the corner he was trying in his own meagre way to bring whatever little happiness he could in the lives of the children of an orphanage.

For a long time I kept thinking, what matters is not your position or your monetary strength to do charity. What matters is that fire within which can get kindled seeing the sorrows of others. What matters is the realisation that someone else needs your help, as you did once. What matters is the feel of that hurt which you may have felt had you been rejected then. The reaching out to those who don't know you at all, gives that wholesome satisfaction which can come by, only when you learn to stand in their shoes.

68: ASPECT of LIFE***THE APPLE

Why is it, the 'apple' has always been the chosen one amongst all the fruits gifted by nature. It's history of having raided mankind can be traced back to the time when God created man and woman, viz., Adam and Eve.

They tasted the 'forbidden apple' and thus began the human saga of happiness and sorrow. It invaded the realm of science when Newton seeing an 'apple' falling from a tree, landed on the law of gravity. Lovers sing to the tune of "You are the apple of my eyes," and thereby emotions get seeped in the world of imagination and love. That naughty mistletoe creeps on the 'apple tree', its berries cuddled betwixt its leaves, giving the right to kiss, to those who stand beneath their beauty. "Oh! You are no better than a rotten apple!" and watch the tears as they roll down, defying the beauty of cheeks 'as red as an apple'. "An apple a day keeps the Doctor away", so 'apples' are givers of good health, and subsequently those 'red cheeks like apples' steal the show. The last, but not the least, 'apple', which finally took over like a hurricane the 'web-world.'

A world which has brought so much within the easy reach of so many. 'Apple' was the cause of the generation of mankind and it continues to give a helping hand whenever so needed, little can one fathom it's worth, simply seeing those 'pretty red apples' hanging from a tree.

69: ASPECT of LIFE***CLAQUE

'Claque' is a French word, meaning that group of people who are hired either to applause at a performance or to applause a speaker or to heckle one. This sets me thinking at the significance of flowers showered or shoes thrown and the impact of such on the audience who have spent time and money to be a part of the audience. How the psyche is bought is definitely some food for thought. An obnoxious play may go jam-packed, thanks to the raving applause, bought. An ordinary speaker can be hyped over and a speaker with substance may be nowhere simply because he had his values stand by him. Quite a vicious circle to deal with and to reckon with.

Can you blame the 'claque', after all it's doing the job it's been paid for? Can you blame the producer of the play, everyone wants its baby to be worth an applause? What bugs me are the rotten eggs thrown at a speaker for absolutely no fault of his, simply to run him down by making his speech appear an apology of a speech, the merit drowned under the 'booing' and the 'pelting of eggs'. On the other hand, the adversary who may be worth all the 'rotten eggs' given an adulation, an adulation bought. As always and everywhere, money shows its power, mostly with those who have nothing else, worth the boast.

70: ASPECT of LIFE***CEMETERY

Now this may sound a lot morbid but cemeteries do fascinate me, maybe because of their mystic spell or because I pause to reflect over the life of those buried there. What must have that person so buried looked like? How did life deal with him or her? How was he or she as a human being and innumerable more, simply make belief conjectures, which hold me mesmerised as to the mysteries of life.

The quietude hanging in the air, undoubtedly give me goose-bumps, but my heart bleeds at the sight of a mother whose come to light a candle at the grave of her departed daughter, or a son with a bouquet of orchids in remembrance of his mother, whose no more. The tombstones, a glaring reminder of how transient life is, and how everything comes to nought. Burnt candles, wilted flowers, tears once dropped and now frozen, are all reminders of moments snatched to honour memory but life carries on for those left behind.

The epitaphs sometimes give an inkling of the person it's dedicated to, and some do have a good deal of humour betwixt the words . . ."Here lies the body of Mary Devoe . . . Wife of Henry Devoe . . . Tears cannot bring her back . . . So I weep" . . . or . . ."The children of Israel wanted bread . . . And the Lord gave them manna . . . Parson Perry wanted a wife . . . And the Devil gave him Anna." I have maybe been to a cemetery twice in my life and have shared my experiences thus. Undoubtedly mystical things do hold me spellbound, maybe because I happen to be born on the mystical no.13 . . . !

VANDANA SINHA

71: ME***OF YORE

Why is it that the ancient castles and mansions have such a magnetic pull for me, to the extent that I happen to get completely lost in the past, trapped within their walls and relive the glory of the bygone days?

My imagination carries me to those hey times with the corridors alive and vibrant with the laughter of the nobility, the men looking ever so stately in their hats and tuxedo, and the swishing of the ladies flowing gowns with their charming bonnets. The boudoirs with the canopied beds make me blush at the thought of the amorous ventures they must have been a witness to, the beauty behind the veils made to come alive with all it's enchantment, as it must have been beholden to the lover's eyes. The dining table resplendent with the silver cutlery and the Brazilian goblets being clinked to the cheers for the good health of all, the naughty exchange of inviting glances, comments to be revered or thrown aside, a mischievous giggle hushed at the slight warning cough coming from the head of the table, must have been so lively, adding volumes to the courses served. The palatial grounds with their old oak and elm trees, where the coy face partially hidden under the parasol must have made many a hearts flutter at the sight of such blossoming looks. The enticing mistletoe creeping on that ancient oak tree, couldn't surely have bided its time till Christmas to give shelter to many a stolen kisses.

The castles and the mansions start to breathe, as though again. My vibrant imagination, cuddling me in its lap, brings the past with such heavenly strokes into the present, that the present becomes a living past.

110

72: ME***'THE DIE-HARD'

"... we regret to inform you ... will be expelled from school ..." A sealed letter from Christ Church College was delivered to my father one fine day after two warnings. His chagrin knew no bounds, and he well fathomed the school's desperate attempts to tame his spoilt and pampered daughter, and the utter desperation and compulsion under which the Principal must have been compelled to send one such.

Anything and everything which was beyond the strict rules as per discipline of the school had to be broken by me, the outcome would be faced anyhow. Who cared for anything, so long the surmounting urge to do something was done with. Getting punished in front of the entire school for talking endlessly during assembly was of course the day's beginning. Disturbing the class by my never ending chatter, with the desk top opening and closing, not for keeping or taking out books, but to talk behind its safety or to somehow smother my giggles which would burst out at the 'drop of a hat.' Plucking mangoes from the trees was a strict offence, and the stricter the regulation, the greater the fun in daring to break it. Another round to the Principal's office, punishment and mounting punishments, outside the Principal's office or the class, mattered not. Complaints by the dozen on the 'parents-teachers meet' and the ensuing scoldings at home, were like throwing 'water on a duck's back'. Not to talk of the subsequent tantrums thrown by me, after the scoldings had closed down. Anyway this letter once again found my parents making their way to my school and I really don't know how my father was able to placate the Principal behind closed doors, as I nonchalantly stood outside in the corridor, waiting to be told, "No more books and no more studies" much to my glee but this never was told and I was mercilessly made to keep clearing exams till I became a Masters in English Literature. The Readers and Professors of my Post Graduate classes too must have heaved a sigh of relief seeing me with my degree in hand. You see "old habits never die."

73: ASPECT of LIFE***HOLDING HANDS

This year 2012 stands to say goodbye, to be amongst one of those innumerable years hidden in the smoggy past. To believe that all that's gone into the past need hold no meaning, is an assumption I'm not in agreement with. My life stands testimony to the treasures I have treasured to build upon, to learn from, to introspect and retrospect and then to gather into my arms what need be gathered and let the rest be sprinkled to be blown away by the breeze.

My empty hours get lost in the smiles and the tears as they come forth again to lightly caress my senses, carrying me into those moments I loved to cling upon, with those who meant to me so much more, than I mean to myself. Each year compressed into my mind with its own significance to stand by, a lesson here and a lesson there, a hand so lovingly holding and guiding mine, cruelly ripped away, leaving me, with each ripping away, more and more alone, each tear making a stronger me. The years rewinding like a camera of life, displaying the characters amidst their settings and me so much a part of it all. All those whom I doted upon to distraction come alive, as though never had they left my side and I so happy and beaming to be holding their hands once again.

Nevertheless paths as though configure at one pinnacle point, that point from which stems the present moment, giving the direction for the future, but it matters not to me, for a simple ticking of the clock making that moment a part of the past. Years carry on, gliding ever so smoothly, one into another and will till my last breath but though a part of the past, never will their presence, be lost to me . . . simply because they have become a part of the past.

74: ME***THAT HUMAN CONNECT

He left for the heavenly realms about five years back and I miss him no less than I miss my parents because though not related to me by blood, I was attached to him vide that human connect which many a times supersedes the love and care of those who may, by fluke of birth, be so related.

He came as a help to my parents when he was barely ten years old, and I breathed my first into this world only a few years later. I always remember him as being like a member of the family, taking care of everyone's needs, asked for or unasked for. His affection by no means any less than my parents, the only one who could dare show his disapproval when I would stick out that mulish chin of mine, more often than not. His every moment dedicated towards our well being and ours equally to his. Squatting cross legged on the floor of his room, many a times would I, big eyed, with ever such alert ears, listen to his stories of fairies and ghosts.

If he happened to be visiting his village, during my visit to Lucknow post marriage, there was no way that I wouldn't see to his being there before my arrival, the visit would be so deprived of its complete happiness without him also around.

How he doted on my sons, tears often welled up in my eyes, as I would see him spoil and pamper them, with a love and attachment so rare. He had nothing to give me and yet he gave me that which only my parents gave me, a complete surrender of love so loving in its selflessness, the most enriched gift no treasure can buy.

Yes to him will I always remain his "Bitiya Rani" and to me will he ever remain my "Baldeo". Let this be a tribute to him, let this be in the warm memory of him, who proved the mystery of that 'human connect'.

75: ME***PASSION

Everyone is passionate about something or the other . . . ranging from one end of the earth to the other. This passion is overpowering, time and space holds no meaning, to it's intoxicating milieu. The soul is at peace, the happiness killing, oblivious to the surroundings, just me and my passion.

A fountain as though exploding within me, unaware from where and how the thoughts and words keep spilling endlessly holding on to the brimming passion within. My atoms caring not how they will be accepted or rejected by those around. Simply because they are pure like the dewdrops glistening on those flowers, as free as the birds and the bees. If hugged by some, the feel is as beautiful, if rejected by some even then it hurts not, because they are mine, to give me, that euphoric feel.

How and when one comes to grips with this energy within is again a matter of time. Hasn't it been rightly said "There is a time and tide for everything." When the time is come there is nothing that can straddle it, it gallops on unharnessed, with the mane flowing smoothly, the bidders bidding by the millions, but it cares not . . . because my passion is a treasure, invaluable, beyond the comprehension of those, who have it not.

76: ME***CHANGING OF TRACKS

Changing tracks in life is decidedly not an easy phenomenon and whether it will be a cake-walk, remains to be seen. This changing of tracks is not as though an overnight process. A great deal of one's self goes into it, at times leaving one in tatters.

The first visible sign is when that feeling of joy goes out, fear starts to take hold and questions begin to grip the mind. It's a phase which can be described as being 'in the doldrums' for one really is in a state of such flux, so as to fathom what will be right or wrong by one's standard, becomes a difficult proposition. Suddenly one fine day one realises that the road has been crossed to the other side and all the cobwebs have been left behind. The feet as though start to walk immediately on that other side of the road. Gradually and very gradually footsteps start finding their footholds, one's self-esteem starts to rear its head, the faith takes a firm hold, bringing back that deserted joy, and the path ahead seems ever so clear, dispelling off whatever doubts or questions which had hitherto been racking the mind. An angelic peace descends and then that complete surrender of self and all. My shoulders free of any baggage, for He is there cradling me in his arms, like His baby . . . as I rest with that joy and cheer in my heart. (I have changed tracks in my life once, because I do not think it mandatory to blindly follow the baggage imposed on me by birth. What matters is eventually my happiness and peace, and for which I am answerable to no one but Him to whom I look upon as my Father in Heaven.)

77: ME***CHRISTMAS

Christmas is just round the corner and each time I get that special feel of happiness. There is something so pure and cosy about the whole festival. The single minded devotion and the preparations, awaiting the birth of Jesus never fail to enchant me.

The singing of the Christmas carols in the light of the candles, making the manger for His arrival, the busy hands in the kitchen getting things together, specially the Christmas cake and the Turkey and of course last but not the least, the Christmas tree, resplendent with the twinkling stars, angels and so many other charms to bring it forth. All the love and care which goes into picking the gifts for the near and dear ones.

It all takes me back to my school days, when I would spend the Christmas day with one friend or the other. Dressed in my pinafore and ballerina shoes, and carrying a well wrapped gift, all starry eyed would I go, drinking to the lees every moment spent there. Can still recall standing as though mesmerised before the Christmas tree, wishfully hoping, "If only a real angel could fly from the tree and take me unto it's glimmering wings." The feeling inside me so Heavenly, with all those stars in my eyes, with that dreamy smile playing on my lips, the whole of me in the grip of my dreams, to the resounding chiming of the Church bells, beckoning the birth of Jesus.

78: ME***GERMANY

It seems as though the ghost of Hitler still stalks the streets of Germany, which appears ever so forlorn and coldly deserted. It was a weird sort of a sensation which crept into my bones, everything seemed so perfect but where was that human feel? Like being in a graveyard, with things written just right on the tombstones, still that feel of clammy fingers around.

There are however just about a couple of things which stand out in my mind. I was enamoured by that fluffy, hand-sized 'pocket dog' in a lady's basket. Oh! It looked so cute with its head bobbing up and down, like a toy dog. The other are the cat-calls I had to encounter in a shopping place once, and my hostess gripping my hand, quickly shoving me into a cab, and heaving a sigh of relief as we speeded off. That was the only time I was awakened to the feeling of the Germans having a heart somewhere. Hitler's Hitlerism has undoubtedly left its mark all around, what with the fading population and the government paying handsomely towards the birth of each new baby and the streets still crying in loneliness.

79: ME***BEYOND

Was not in the least familiar with the diverse ways of life, having been brought up in the lap of luxuries by my parents. My breaths throughout confined to a fairy-tale's unravelling of days, where everything was textured with poised laughter, not even aware that there could be a life, a life other than the one I was blissfully breathing in.

All the protective folds started to fall apart after my marriage, bringing me face to face with the glaring realities of what days and nights are actually made up of. I handled, I mishandled, but grappling all the same and each blow made me the stronger for the next one, as though lurking around the corner. Each time I hauled myself up, simply refusing to throw up my hands in the face of what my perspective of situations told me to be right. A re-play of the Battle of Waterloo chequered my life, sometimes a winner and at other times a loser, but never a coward. My pages of literacy stared getting laced with the education of life.

A personality which had been so blind to the sound of the footsteps of others began to open up, to those sobs, to those grimy hands, to those wanting eyes, to those unspoken words, to the deep realisation that there is a always a shadow of someone around the corner who perhaps needs my hug or simply that look of understanding, which also is denied to him.

80: ASPECT of LIFE***CHARITY

"Let not thy left hand know what thy right hand doeth." Nowadays charity is not simply a secret betwixt the hands. In fact charity ceases to be charity if it's not brought to the world's notice. Not only brought to notice but brought amidst a great deal of fanfare, in the glare of the camera lights, the paparazzi doing their fulfilling rounds, and of course the media hype not far behind. The takers with their heads bowed and of course the givers thinking themselves no less than God or at best a demi-God in the making. To be honest the receivers of alms have equally degraded themselves. They are prepared to demean themselves to any extent possible in order to be a recipient of whatever much or less, they can lay their hands on.

Its further seen to be deciphered whether the cause for the charity is done justice to, or whether all the money in the name of charity makes its way stealthily into their private coffers. An extremely vicious circle indeed, a cobweb in which both the giver and the receiver are pathetically caught, none the better for the other. Both the right and the left hands giving, and both the hands receiving, a laudable action, caught in the cameras, for eternity.

81: ASPECT of LIFE***THE RED CARPET

The wedding altar, the beginning of history. History rolled into the folds of the red carpet. The fusion of two souls by the promises made via repetition of the Pastor's voice, by the religious rites performed. The smiles resplendent with the happiness singing from the chiming of the Church bells. The diamond flaunting its glitter from the wedding ring, speaking of so much warmth and love. Sprinkling of the Holy Water on the newlyweds and then finally the lifting of the veil, to reveal the shy anticipation in those eyes, the blushing cheeks, and the radiant beauty, all encompassed within the warmth of the virgin kiss. Entering the Church holding on to the father's arm and leaving it, clasping the hands of the groom, leaving the threshold of the Church to be carried across the threshold of the new house.

The flowing bridal dress and the veil, their laughter merging with the spilling glee from the lips, mark the entry into a new life. A life so secret till that moment, begins to unfold chapter after chapters of smiles and tears. The vow of 'till death do us apart' and the 'wedding ring' a constant and a repeated reminder of the years spent, each by the other's side, to stay bound together or to drift apart, depending on the 'history rolled into the folds of the red carpet.'

82: ASPECT of LIFE***LOST MOMENTS

It's strange, at the time of marriage both the partners are so perceptive of one another's virtues and failings, mental and physical both. The good and the bad, gradually and inadvertently start to leave their marks, the laughter lines or the forehead furrow, unnoticed. Earlier nothing that escaped the eyes seemed to have waved a hasty goodbye and everything starts to de-friend those one's ever so vigilant eyes. The pain and the happiness, the wrinkles, the greying hair, the shuffling steps, the lost aspirations in the eyes, the craving for attention, all seem to get buried under the mantle of 'taken for granted', at both the ends.

Compliments wait to be showered on others . . . the pleasures and pain of the rest, never fail to bring forth the "A-ha" or "O-ho", arms reach out to fulfil the dreams of all and sundry. In short the heart cries or laughs at the mercy of others. Surely comes the day whence either of the one bids the final goodbye. It's then, the heart cries, for the valuable spells lost under the wrinkles and the grey hair, it's then the heart cries for the holding of hands with that reassuring squeeze, it's then the heart cries for the warmth of each other's bodies.

Alas, isn't it too late in the day when the body so cold has nothing left to give but a remembrance of those seconds which got lost in those years of togetherness and still 'never together'.

VANDANA SINHA

83: ME***U.S.A./AMERICA

During my visit to New York I was a lot taken aback by the hurried steps all around. It seemed as though America was competing with the rest of the world, to be ahead, as in everything else. Blank faces, all around, as though vying with time, with the skyscrapers against the skyline. A country of immigrants, it can little boast of a defined culture but the self-created culture does give way to a liveliness, not chaperoned by the do's and the don'ts. Friendliness waves in the air as much as obesity throngs the eating joints. Though most Americans come across as if a little laden in the head, in most cases than not its simply an eyewash, for they well can fathom, which side 'their bread is buttered'. It's a pleasure though to see faces of differing origins, all breathing pretty openly in the same American air, with the same civil rights.

All the coasts, with their own scenic beauty and the flora and fauna, the best which appealed to me, being the southern coast, it's Hawaii Island with its rocking palm trees. Standing ahead by way of its economy and political clouts, it seems like America has made its place on the face of the global world.

84: ME***THE BRUNETTES

So I realised, there are 'orange Irish' and the 'green Irish' . . . the Irish Catholics being the former and the Irish Protestants the latter. Ireland, a quaint island in Europe, which appeared much like England by way of its landscapes. Strange though, that the Irish screw up their faces at the mention of the English and vice-versa, each thinking themselves superior to the other. The Irish have an extremely marked accent when they speak English and I remember, with all my wonder for phonetics, I had picked it up quite well. It's mostly a flaming red all around, what with most Irish being brunettes. The pockets go heavy on drinks, the Irish capacity to hold as many as seven pegs, would hold me dumb-struck. They hold the British beauty at par, endowed with equally sharp features. Cork, took me down memory lane, since all our nuns in Loreto Convent happened to be from Cork. Can never forget their fresh 'chicken in the basket', which never fails to bring that appetising flavour back. The 'orange' and the 'green', the 'Irish' and the 'British' may keep cold shouldering each other, but none can do without the other.

85: ME***THE FRENCH

Bonjour! The French will be French by all dimensions. As snobbish as the British, if not more, with an exaggerated pride in their race and their French language. During my visit there I found them to be madly possessive about their language, so much so they would draw a complete blank when I spoke English, though it is well whispered that they can understand English enough, to help guide a tourist find the way, but they think it below their dignity to so much as nod their head in the presence of the English language. My smattering of French helped me like 'the light of a torch in the alleys'. Their basic nature I found to be rude and curt, their waiters arrogant and shops unfriendly. The night life in Paris was, of course, by no means any the less, for all that I had heard it being acclaimed for. The flowing grace and the elegance with which the night shows were performed, put nudity on a pedestal of beauty, not the least bit touched by vulgarism. Their Louvre Museum held me spellbound by the works of the maestros of art, the French acclaimed for their willing appreciation of the female contours on the billowy side. The market square with their sculptural effects stood unmatched to any that I may have been a witness to. Their champagne happens to be the only drink, I have enjoyed so far, it's smooth tingling touch down the throat, with it's pretty levelled intoxicating after effect, I still smile with at the remembrance. The French, though they are called 'frogs' definitely deserve no such nomenclature, they do stand out as a race, if not at par with the British, at least as a race which has its own kaleidoscopic effects, against the musical energy of the French language. Au revoir . . . !

86: ME***THE STIFF-UPPER-LIPPED

My sojourns overseas, to a lot many countries, have been an eye-opener to the various facets of the human genre. My maiden venture took me to England, the only country which gave me goose-bumps when I stepped on to Heathrow.

Was a lot familiar with the cultural effects of this country, having grown up reading and subconsciously living in its environment within the pages of books and stories. The people truly British with a great deal of pride for their race, the stiff-upper-lipped, flat phrase concluding it all. Of course there is no denying the fact that the British do have their own much defined culture, which makes them stand apart. Their etiquette unsurpassed viz., its ice-cold formality, nonetheless charismatic and distinguished, a certain fixed norm to be followed for each occasion. Their sharp intellect speaks through their normally piercing eyes, and their sense of decorum in no way allows them the leverage of showing their real feelings in a hitting manner, always politely warm if not cold, depending as and when.

England is decidedly a hub of literary figures, whose classical footholds still stand unmatched. The meadows with their maids and cows reflected the pictures in books, I had been a witness to. Was enamoured by the cosy, warm pretty cottages with their flowery gardens and the crackling fireplace. The old castles with their expansive grounds never failed to bring into mind the royal figures, resplendent in their flowing gowns and the men with their tail-coats and hats, as they would have made their way around. The parasitic Mistletoe as it crawled on to an old oak tree, in the castle ground had made me rub my hands with that childish glee. Sir Walter Scott's novels of the Knights and the ladies, would take hold of my imagination, as also my awareness that the England which had hitherto been compressed in books and my ever vivid imagination, was in no where lacking, by way of its truly British essence.

87: ME***OH! THOSE HINDI CLASSES . . .

If there was one subject in school I was really proficient at, well then it was Hindi. So much so, my parents were called to be made aware of the gruesome reality that if required steps were not taken it would take little for me to plug in my Intermediate class, since failing in Hindi would be failing all together, it being a compulsory subject. Started the quest for a person who could tutor me in Hindi. Five expectant teachers came and, after no less than a couple of days, never showed their faces again. My father somehow got hold of a sixth one who, it seemed, took up the challenging job of at least getting me through with the bare minimum of forty percent.

Much as I would try all the tricks possible to somehow get a day's respite from that 'one horrible hour' (an hour I simply dreaded) dedicated to only Hindi and Hindi, none would work out, since my parents knew me inside out. There would sit my teacher across the table and I would sit with my head turned mulishly sideways. The last ten years papers were consulted and a questionnaire was prepared by my tutor. The essay held twenty marks and he put his finger on the topic '*nauka vihar*' (boat ride), and made me cram it up from the beginning till the end. Sure enough, as I opened the question paper, it winked at me. Oh! Twenty marks were in my pocket, and I started off "It was a moonlit night, since it was '*amavasaya*' and . . ." That evening, my tutor's happiness knew no bounds as he asked me to relate and the moment he heard '*amavasaya*' (moonless night) instead of '*poornima*' (moonlit night) he literally squirmed in his chair, while I looked the other way round. Suffice it to say, I did barely scrape through my Hindi paper.

Thanks to the tolerance, patience and endurance of my Hindi tutor and thanks also to my tolerance, patience and endurance of somehow managing to sit through that one dreadful hour, where every second was devoted to only Hindi, what if I sat through with my head turned the other way round.

88: ME***WAS IT?

Many a times have I pondered over a question which gnaws at my mind. Is my life a 'carry-on' of my previous life, in which I was perhaps in some way related with England? It's not without reason that I think so.

My Mummy used to relate to me, how 'Dury' the English nurse who was in attendance, when I breathed my sweet-little-first into this world, was insistent upon adopting me, simply because I looked no less than an English baby. (In my family in Lucknow, childbirths took place at home.) So I feel it all started from there. Even as a child I had an Anglican bent of mind. To my Papa's utter consternation, all my friends happened to be Anglo-Indians. I would only speak in English, read English, dress English, sing only English songs, with just the right amount of 'lilts' here and there and do nothing short of everything that had an English touch. The fascination for the church always was and still is there. So much so, I even have a deep desire to be buried, and have expressed my wish as much. Why is it that amongst the four siblings I happen to be the only one, with this 'penchant', for most things which are downed with an English flavour, when all of us were brought up amidst the same infrastructure?

Sometimes I crave to come across someone who could take me into my past life or what one calls 'past life regression'. Many will ask me "Why?" I really don't have a graphic answer. Maybe it'll explain a lot of missing links in my life, maybe my gut instinct that certain things which are left unfulfilled get fulfilled in this lifetime or simply to realise that my subconscious is a platform of the past, giving a face to my past, present and future.

89: ASPECT of LIFE***FEELINGS

Feelings are like ripples in the water. Their flow is endless, taking to high and low tides, beyond your control, beyond your comprehension. They keep branching out, some with withering leaves, some with flowers and a lot many with fruits. To try blocking them would be like killing a part, so much of yourself. It's easier said than done, to do away with negative feelings or try converting them into positive ends. Perhaps sages are bestowed with that remarkable energy to overpower all things negative or to convert the negative into positive.

My experiences have taught me to allow the feelings to flow, naturally, unhindered, time and turnings will either do the required pruning or will allow them to stabilise or nip them at an opportune time. Is it humanly possible to control the surge of pleasure you feel at the sight of a budding rose, or refuse to let the fragrance of an enamouring perfume raise your spirits, or close your eyes to the entrancing beauty of an enticing lady? Again is it within one's reach not to let your eyes well-up at the remembrance of someone you loved to distraction and have lost or hold on to your bearings at the small and big happenings in every-day life or to love even if your heart refuses to accept? Not so easy to always look at the pinker side of things and to shoo the blues away. To be positive and never to let negativity creep in.

I'm a victim of my feelings. I let them ripple my being, with their feathery touch. They make me laugh and cry, as and when, they make me ever so enamouring or ever so despicable, to some, they make me love with all my heart or make me turn my face with all my might because I look upon myself as that 'enchanting wild rose in the wood', which, if it can weather a storm, it can also spread it's dainty fragrance amidst the enchantment of the wood.

90: ASPECT of LIFE***THE GHOST WRITERS

Many a times the term 'ghost writers' has aroused a kind of curiosity in my mind, perhaps because 'ghosts' never fail to kindle that mystical feel in me. Had wondered umpteen times as to why writers do 'ghost writing', till I happened to lay my hands on an article on them, and learnt how lucrative this venture is.

I'm aware, there are innumerable celebrities and others who have scant time to usher in a book on their own and so they hire 'ghost writers' to pen on their behalf. The books get floated in the market under the hirer's name, getting all the acclaim, while the actual claimant of all the wonderful reviews, stays hidden betwixt the personal throbbings of the pages. Emoting for those whom you don't know from Adam, ruffling the moments of their lives, those seeped in failures or glory, those clandestine affairs enjoyed for keeps, or lost amidst the layers of the comforters, sieving from the political gambles, to be projected or not to be, must be quite a mental jig-saw puzzle.

Still so many, so adept at the art of writing, take up this challenge, because of all the wealth it gives. They sell their 'art' to bring others into the limelight, while they remain hidden in the folds of secrecy forever, while they see the books being raved over and modestly being accepted by the 'so-called-writer'.

It sure needs a 'big-big heart' to be a mute witness to the laurels falling into the laps of those, who deserve them not. The laurels which are rightfully that of the 'ghost-writer'. I do bow my head in regard for them, for though I'm an amateur writer I'm well aware of all the effort that goes in. An effort which is such a pleasure, to be seen as your 'baby'.

VANDANA SINHA

91: ME***IN BIHAR

Having spent my pre-marriage days in Lucknow or the neighbouring cities, coming to Bihar for the first time after my marriage, did make me realise that state boundaries do exist, vide culture, language, the mental make-up and, of course, the flora and fauna.

Gone to the winds were 'the *nafaasat* and the *nazaakat*' and 'the *takalluf* of Lucknow. Everything seemed so much, taken for granted. The mental make-up so complex, as to leave me completely at bay, trying to figure out what could be taken at face value, and what could be not and still being unable to come to a conclusive conclusion.

Crossing the language barrier was as Herculean a task. The locals could hardly understand my chaste Hindi tongue and would land up saying "*ka kahatini?*" My mind would go racing as to how best I could make them understand my simple language. Subconsciously I found myself registering Bhojpuri and it started to make its maiden venture now and then. The most convenient word I picked up was "*ethi*", for I found its usage in abundance. Whenever I was at a loss for the right word I'd use "*ethi*" as a scapegoat, like "*suna u ethi le awa na*" and sure enough the message would go across like lightning.

Today I find myself as proficient in Bhojpuri as an outsider can best be. The birds and the bees . . . and the green habitation here, does enamour me, like always.

Lucknow will always remain an epitome of its culture with language and Bihar will always remain Bihar with its plus and minus. The biggest plus being its unmatched capacity for teaching "*ethi*" to all those who step in here. Like it or lump it.

92: ME***THESE GREY HAIR

Oh! These strands of 'grey hair'. Are not they tied together with 'fairy-tale-ribbons', bouncing up and down, as they yearn to tell stories, no book can swear by, gathered from the pages of life, to be shared, with the minutes ticking by. The respect which comes forth, if for nothing else, as a mark of regard for age and the subsequent seniority it claims.

At least our government has the good sense to dole out that much reverence by way of giving some added advantages to the senior citizens. What sets my grey-cells nudging each other is the very simple question "Why do we take such pains to hide the strands of wisdom and respect?" We humans are so vain, that we will go to all lengths to camouflage our advancing age marks, ever look ever sweet sixteen, even if our legs are half way down the grave. No stone is left unturned, colouring by all means, the easiest to come by. Applications and re-applications follow, since the proud grey syndrome takes a good deal of pride in showing itself off. A fortnight of bidding it bye and there it starts peeping, making its presence felt the more and dump everything and make a bee-line to the ever waiting parlours.

I say, let these charming 'grey hair' crown you with their glory. Why hide their beauty with phials of artificiality? I say, when will I redeem myself from the green leaves of 'henna', if only to let my 'grey hair', tell their stories of yore . . . ?

93: ME***AN 'EMOTIONAL FOOL' . . . TO BE RECKONED WITH

"Enjoy everything that happens in your life but never make your happiness dependent on an attachment to any person, place or thing," so said Wayne Dyer, the American author and motivational speaker. I call myself an 'emotional fool' because I land up doing precisely this and the separation thenceforth makes me so emotionally bankrupt at least for a while. Tears well up at the mere thought and make me wonder at my emotional fragility. It's me who undergoes the pain. Do those whom these tears revere also feel the pang? Now am I not putting my expectation on a reciprocal level, something I have no business to do.

Each a victim of one's own failings, the extent varying according to one's personal linings. What sets me thinking is the source of that insurmountable strength which towers over me in a moment of crisis, making me counter it with a wisdom and tenacity, which seems so foreign to my hitherto 'emotional foolery'. I have delved into my 'emotional labyrinths', and strangely each time I have come up with the same revelations. Its these very 'emotion auto atoms' which are the givers, so unobtrusively, by way of my 'deep emotional bonding', to my lineage, to my parents flawless upbringing of me, to my distinctive education, all culminating in that respect not only for myself but also for all those deserving of such. Even if that person happens to be a beggar, a beggar in clothing, but a treasured person by way of character. Damn those tears and damn my 'emotional foolery'. Let them fall in remembrance of those who deserve so much more. Who have that rare quality and presence of 'wetting my kerchief', with their goodness.

94: ME***A REVERIE

These few past days have had me rolling amidst a gamut of heart breaking emotions, as I made my way to Lucknow to be there for the first departed anniversary of Mummy. Agonising yet with a smile, to celebrate and not to mourn for the life of one who was an icon of the best by which life is to be lived by. Mummy will always be there, her presence in life as potent, as her pervading presence despite her absence. On our way back home we broke our journey at Tilouthu (my husband's village home). Thirty long years have flitted by since I stepped into this house as a young, pretty coy bride, so naive, like a blossoming flower, blissfully unaware of the storms which would threaten to rip it apart, as and when.

As I sit in the veranda tonight, a smile plays around my lips, as feelings and emotions out number each other. Tides have come and tides have ebbed, but none have been able to sweep me off my feet. None have been able to mar me of my inner beauty which still shines forth, unable to veil my prettiness or grace. None have been able to charm away my childishness which still claps its hands now and then. A person sitting in the same veranda, thirty-six years later, so sure of herself, so much more strong, yet the wisdom shining through her eyes cannot hide the impishness which smiles, that impish smile.

95: ME***FACEBOOK

When I signed in with Facebook, little did I realise what I was getting into. I was totally at bay, as though all the ends were hanging loose. Initially I was like a nomad, dropping in to say 'hello' once in a blue-moon. After my Mummy left for the other realm in November last year, my pen started to beckon me again, after a hiatus of almost two decades. My parents' voice started falling in my ears asking me to write, since they always felt that I had a flair for it.

Inadvertently I found myself giving shape to my thoughts on my Facebook 'wall'. All my write-ups, a tribute to my ever doting Papa and Mummy who made me thus capable. Gradually I started visiting the home pages of my friends and my eyes started opening up to a lot of facets of those on my friend's list, or rather a deeper understanding, some for the better and some for the worse. My page became resplendent with my, mostly satirical writings, hitting out on aspects of life which glare at me, be it day or be it night, made meaningfully colourful with links . . . shared.

Facebook is an enticing world of its own. Each tries to give forth whatever he or she is best at. Always projecting a molly-coddle image of oneself, scared of coming forth with anything which will not show them at their real best, a book with a hard-bound-cover. There are a handful of friends like me, who care a damn, about their reflection in the light of, what I would call public opinion and keep moving on. I have the thread ends well in hand now and have learnt the Facebook art of 'connecting' with like-minded people, whose pages are vibrant with awakenings of sorts.

96: ASPECT of LIFE***SPARING OF NONE . . .

Time and tide waits for none and neither does age. Every year takes away or adds to your span. Who doesn't want to spend one's life in the cradle being taken care of by those 'soft hands' and catching winks to the hum of a lullaby, with not a care in the world? Does life put up hands there? No it takes you through the full gamut of cycles, you are destined to go through.

Days dance into your 'teens' with rainbows all around. Soon, without your realising it, steps have climbed onto adulthood and life starts from here in the true sense of the word. You are left at the mercy of your own abilities and the learnings of the past, become your tutor for the future. Your past has chiselled your character and it's up to your good sense at how best you are able to put it into use. Old age is not too far away and it's days are packed to overflowing with experiences, wisdom, and memories. The final end spares none and sooner or later you find yourself at the threshold of life's end, the same as you had found yourself at the threshold of life. A cycle of life, complete, in a circle, affirming the number zero.

97: ASPECT of LIFE***
AT ONE'S NAKED BEST . . .

I heard somewhere, if you tie the tail of two cats, they don't get united. Their basic tendency of yapping at one another, will certainly not change, by simply trying to keep them together. No matter what the circumstances the basic nature of the person always stays for keeps.

You meet a suave dandy, who seems to be nowhere lacking, either in appearance or demeanour. A waiter passing by spills a drink on his coat, by mistake. His immediate reaction will bespeak his innate character. A simple shrug of the shoulder with a light brush away of the fallen drops will bespeak of the person's inborn sophistication. Another will, without the blink of an eye, start abusing the waiter for his clumsiness and subsequently vitiate the surrounding. This coarse outburst, is that person's inherent temperament, which comes to the fore, at the 'drop of a hat'.

Life is a flow of situations some favourable and vice-versa, handled or mishandled, bringing forth one's reality on the screen. It has been wisely said, "A person is best judged in moments of crisis" because the clothing falls apart leaving the person at his naked best.

98: ASPECT of LIFE***THE TRAIN JOURNEY

A train journey is so akin to the journey of life. It starts from a station and finally ends at its final destination. The same way as the beginning and the end of life. Stations, all through the way, none like the other, the turning points, each so variant. Passengers getting in and getting out, make friends with some and strangers others, the innumerable people who come and go out of our lives, leaving their mark or none at all. The speed slowing and gaining again, the pace of life, never steady. As the train moves on, the scenic view of the 'flora and fauna', holds one spellbound but the train keeps gliding forward, unaffected, the dreams of a person, but life keeps moving by. Some travel in the general class or the 3 tier, while the more privileged in the air-conditioned compartments, as the pocket of each one permits, the different strata of society each living according to one's means. Confined to the berth, as one is confined to the dwelling place. Getting down at the destination and there the journey ends, as also one day will end the journey of life.

99: ASPECT of LIFE***THE BARTENDER

A 'bartender' is a man's best friend. He alone knows the state of a man's mind when he frequents a bar and he has a remarkable knack of knowing how that mood is to be tackled.

Just the right drink, with the right presentation. Patiently lending an ear to the person's woes and the innumerable trials which have made his life their home. Coming out with just the right exclamations, as and when required. Swiftly, without being asked, refilling the glass to be downed again and again, till the person reaches the level of satiation, and gets the euphoric feeling, that nobody's life could be better than his. A heavy tip to the 'bartender' for being a 'friend in need' and stumbles out with a satisfied smile on his face. Gone are the scowl and the feeling of hopelessness.

Gets up the next morning with a terrible hangover, distraught and lost. The evening again sees him making his way to his favourite bar where the 'bartender' is all set for the replay, just the right amount of everything at just the right time, the happy smile and the 'happy wave' as he swaggers out, into the night.

100: ASPECT of LIFE***
BEYOND CONTROL . . .

When certain things are beyond your control, the wisest thing to do is to accept them gracefully, as your lot, and work on how to turn them to your advantage. Fighting them will certainly not lead you anywhere. It'll only lead to making its presence felt even the more. Endeavour to change yourself so as to make yourself more adaptable, more lovingly understanding and more empathetic.

It's easier said than done because you will be the only one stepping forward again and again, surely leading to frustration endless and a grinding feeling of hopelessness. However soon you'll find yourself settling down to it as a way of life with no conscious effort required after a point. The status quo, remains the same, neither more nor less, only the perspective has changed, the modus operandi has changed, giving a new face to the problem. Looked upon now not as 'something beyond your control' but as something 'well under your control'. Simply because you have accepted it and tackled it the right way.

101: ME***OH THIS ADDICTION . . .

Writing is an addiction, like any other, the pen keeps waving itself, till you hold and pamper it. It's simply a matter of time, for once the pen is in hand, thoughts start gushing out like water from a waterfall and the pen starts to move on its own. Each word, an emotion spelled out, a feeling related, as the pen keeps getting jostled, happily or tearfully. Years get compressed into heartfelt lines, the past, present and the future, smoothly blended into one. Emotions so strong or mellow, hitting or loving, depending on the flow of the mood. The power of words is immense, they can make or mar, so they need to be handled with delicacy and understanding. What irks me most when lost to the world, with the pen in hand, is to be disturbed due to some reason or the other because the flow gets impaired and that can put one off to a large extent.

Manuscripts have come down through ages and will continue to go down for ages to come. Never will this pen take a respite, so mischievous is it, with its pranks.

102: ASPECT of LIFE***
TO BE OR NOT TO BE . . . ?

It certainly takes something to be honoured as the 'chief guest' of a function. Strangely what holds my attention is not the 'chief guest' but what follows his arrival which holds me spellbound.

The people gathered at the entrance to receive him, each toppling over the other to present a garland or flowers and the 'chief guest' desperately trying to hold on to his composure under their smothering affection. A little smile here and a little smile there unable to decide whether to hold on to his bearings or to the garlands and the flowers. Next comes the 'picture session' and once again each vying with the other as to who will manage to snuggle closest to the 'chief guest', sandwiched in between people he doesn't know from Adam, as if it matters the least whether its Tom, Dick or Harry standing next to him. By the time the function is over the poor person is sucked of all his energy and enthusiasm, reeling under the vapour of so much love and adoration. (As for me, I refuse to be a party to all this fanfare, sitting mutely and marvelling at the idiocy of the people and wondering whether 'good sense' had smartly walked out of the back door.)

103: ASPECT of LIFE***FASHION

'I know it's a fashion statement' but it begs an explanation. The more bizarre the fashion, the bigger an 'Avant-garde' of fashion are you. Torn patches all over the jeans, the larger the patches, the higher the price. Why should the paupers be ashamed of their patched clothing but why not? You see they didn't have to pay a price for it. Clothing in name, mere strips, bashfully trying to hide nothing, the price being paid, is for covering nothing. No need to hang the clothes in the shade, lest the colour goes. The faded patches at the elbow, knees and the calf muscles, is a flaunting of style. I say, why take the trouble of visiting malls, simply make a beggar's wardrobe yours and you will have all that you want, to stand out in a crowd. No barber's training needed now, just hold the scissors anyhow, and go swish-swash and lo and behold the most trendy hair cut is yours for asking and the mousse does the rest. Hair standing on edge like a porcupines, or so long, as to be able to tie a pony, the gender marvellously, a guess game from the rear. The women with strips of hair hanging, all over the face, trying to hide ugliness or beauty, remains to be deciphered. The logic is simple, the bigger the hole made in the pocket, the bigger a specimen. Standing out in a crowd, for looking nothing short of the money spent or gone down the drain.

104: ASPECT of LIFE***SMALL WONDERS

Just look around and marvel at the small wonders, scattered all around, so becoming in their untouched simplicity. The natural hues of the flowers, blossoming at their wedding time, hues which no human palette can create. Their fragrance, as though emanating from a secret source, the Arabian perfumes put to shame. The multitude of birds, drowning the quietude with their endless cacophony of chirping and twittering, their graceful flight a haven for the eyes. The silkworms cuddled in their cocoons, like small balls of baby cotton hanging from the mulberry trees, spinning silk, so fine and soft. The strutting peacock, not the least bit modest as it spreads it's wings to the glory of the sun, doing a ballet worth reviews. The doodle-do of the cock, wishing all a happy morning, by it's own clock. Glitter worms, like stars of the earth, reach out and there is the star in your hand. The flowers waiting impatiently for the colourful butterflies to partake of their sweet nectar. The lacking of the small wonders nowhere, in abundance, only to be caressed and the heavenly beauty to be felt and treasured.

105: ASPECT of LIFE***
THE OTHER SIDE OF THE FENCE . . .

A lifetime is spent in 'peeping at the other side of the fence' never finding the time to glance at your 'side of the fence', always finding the other side greener than yours. Besotted with the feeling that the lackings in your life, are more than in anyone else's, keeps taking your breath away. Blaming God for the lot that has come your way. Cursing your fate for all the mishaps in your life. Wishing for your neighbour's possessions to walk into your house. The wanting endless, whether you need it or not, wanting it simply because your friend has it. Never trying to live within your means, always in that killer's mode for more and more blood at your hands. The desire unquenchable, simply because 'if the others' can have it then why not me?

Never so much as making the mildest effort to glance around and be a witness to the smiles scattered around you, never having the good sense to thank the Almighty, for His mercies, big or small, never ever having the soothing feel of contentment. Never apprehending the day when it will be too late because by then the soft grass which had waited and waited, to feel your footsteps to tread on it, will be dry and coarse, because you were too busy 'peeping on the other side of the fence'.

106: ASPECT of LIFE***BALANCE

This universe rests on the principle of 'balance', tilt the bookcase, just that wee bit, and you'll be a witness to the books sliding off and landing with a crash onto the floor, so also with all the various aspects of life, even the slightest misbalancing effect can create havoc.

Living life to the fullest optimum, in the right manner, according to your understanding of things despite being aware of 'that only truth' and creating that 'balance' is a reflection of one's intelligence. Walking down the path of life, with that bounce in the steps, hob-nobbing and giggling with the flowers, so what if a thorn pricks, now and then, the tear drop will soon dry, making the most of the moments come by despite the awareness of the path meeting it's end at one point is truly what life is all about.

Leaving that path for the others to tread upon, later, amidst your laughter and to the feel of your bouncy footsteps, a whispering guidance, to that 'balancing mystery' of life.

107: ASPECT of LIFE***THE LULLABIES

When two people utter the holy vows of marriage, resulting in the so-called unison of souls, life seems to be nothing short of 'beds and beds of roses', of course minus the thorns. Days fly by seeped in the blissful air of romance and 'dreams come true', couldn't be more enchanting. Limpid eyes bearing souls, heart winning smiles and the electrifying presence of each.

Gradually, in some cases the chemistry, worth a writer's novel starts to buckle at the knees. The sight of one another which, not many hours back, resulted in sighs of wanting suddenly take a u-turn with each wanting to be out of the other's sight. The sound of the voices which hitherto whispered sweet nothings, lose their whispering melody. Compatibility turns to incompatibility and a worse couple could not have been better matched. The never ending 'blame game', bringing each other's sleep to naught.

The unison of two souls, leave their cradle of the altar and find themselves at the threshold of the divorce court for a divorce. Divorce 'the counter word for marriage', and what sprouted as 'till death do us apart' ends with the requiem 'will stay apart till our last breath in peace'. So hats off to 'marriages' and 'divorces', each to sing their own 'lullabies'.

108: ASPECT of LIFE***HANGERS

'Come hail, come storm,' who doesn't want to have a 'clean chit' and so starts the 'hanger syndrome'. Keep shoving the blame onto the shoulders of the most vulnerable victim around, keeping your shoulders light and free. Spoil the poor person's day but liven up yours. Drown his sleep and you snore the night away. Problems in your professional life, hang it around your boss's or your colleague's neck. If a couple have a show down, hang it around each other's fist. If your dog howls, hang it around the clamour in the neighbour's house. Not been successful in a venture, then the destiny is to be hanged. Strange though 'hanged unto death' the capital punishment is fast on its way out but this 'blame hanging' perseveres to perfection. The victim goes around with a 'noose' around his head, from the time the decree is passed without the privilege of a court hearing. The heavy breaths seeping his energy away and as always the real victim prances through his days. Little realising, that soon he'll fall short of 'hangers' but by then it'll too be late to even ask himself the question "Why"? He will then be the one going around with a 'noose around his head', to save himself from his own 'mocking gaze'.

109: ASPECT of LIFE***PROPERTY

Property and assets last through generations and it is this empire, which proves to be the 'swan's last song' regarding the love and caring betwixt the inheritors.

Those siblings who grew up together, sharing the same bed, sharing the same bread, laughing together, wiping away one another's tears, skipping hand in hand, suddenly become sworn enemies, overnight. It's as though, all the hitherto existing love is swept aside for hatred to make its way, in their paths.

What has been the propounder of this holocaust? Of course this overpowering property. Of course these bricks and concrete. Of course the glimmer of all the jewellery. Of course the thick wads of money.

Is the power of love so weak as to be overpowered by such material crumbs? Is love so transient as to be overtaken by lawyers and courts? Is love so illusionary as to be mulled over by abuses and threats? "Yes" This property has the Devil's blessings, to annul it all, in a matter of seconds, where the Devil's sense prevails. Years and generations become the victims of this intoxicating love for property, breaths breathe their last, down years and generations, for what? The realisation never comes to stay, empty handed we come and so we go. All that we leave behind is the shadow of our real selves.

110: ASPECT of LIFE***THE INTRINSIC TRUTH

'Everything changes in the blink of an eye', as I 'bid adieu' to the world, a world I had thought would cease to be, with me not around. In a matter of seconds I'm shifted to the floor and treated worse than an untouchable. I suddenly become a ghost, I who had given the strength to my dear and near ones, to be fearless in life, the worse thing now, is to be left alone in a room with me. I who had been hugged and kissed a second before, now a mere object, entirely at the mercy of those around. The head of the table I used to occupy, though now vacant, the rest of the chairs soon occupied, as none wait for me to sit at the head of the table.

Normalcy starts to waft in the air, as I hover above, wanting to console the tears which fall from the eyes of my loved ones, now and then but there is no pull where I am. I look at my carcass below. Where has vanished the beauty I was indeed so proud of? Is this six feet by six feet, the only place I belong to now? Soon the hearse car arrives and draped in my bridal gown with my bridal veil, which had once been unable to hold the beauty it was veiling, now veils a face deprived of its once pampered beauty. I leave behind everything I had spent a lifetime for. I leave behind even my body, as the coffin is lowered to the sound of the Pastor's voice . . . 'from dust unto dust'. Nothing of me remains, except memories, to be remembered by.

My parents . . . Papa and Mummy

My parents . . . Papa and Mummy

My elder son . . . Anurag, who works as a
Senior Consultant in I.B.M. in U.S.A.

My elder son Anurag

My younger son Vinamra.

My husband and me . . . the innocent, petite,
demure bride, who stepped onto the threshold of marriage
with steps so unsure, little fathoming all that lay ahead.

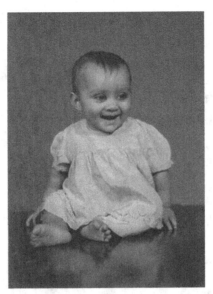

Me . . . this happy, grinning baby, who grew into an endearing, spoilt brat, thanks to all her Papa's pampering.

Me . . . as the bride, soon to step out alone, from the protected arms of my parents, gradually learning about the harsh realities of life.

My younger son and me in our house.

My husband and me.

Me . . . in Singapore.

My husband, younger son and me in Bangkok.

Anurag with Vinamra in his lap in the
garden of my house in Lucknow.

Me as the bride, betwixt the loving folds of my parent's arms.

My ' Fairy House ' in Lucknow . . . my ancestral home ' Chaulakhi ' built by my Grand-father Sir Bisheshwar Nath Srivastava, the second Indian to be the Chief Justice of the Court of Oudh and bestowed with Knighthood thereafter. Betwixt the walls of this house, I blossomed surrounded and protected by the love of my family and the families of 5 Uncles. Every nook and cranny like an inseparable part of my being. Stepping out as a bride was a medley of feelings, as though being torn away from myself and the ambiguous happiness which a young girl of 22 years like me, felt at the thought of marriage. My cradle still rocks in my ' Fairy House ' as did I really grew by way of ' what life is all about ' as I stepped out of my ' Fairy House.'

Me . . . as I look today, having traversed a long length of the journey of life, growing from a spoilt brat into a graceful, middle aged lady, who despite her wisdom, her hazel eyes still twinkle with the impishness of that 'cheeky girl' lurking in her somewhere. A daughter who has done her parent's proud.

Me . . . cheeky grin and the twinkle in the eyes, bringing to nought the umpteen hiccups in my life.

My elder son standing beside one of the many statues
in the garden of my home in Lucknow.

111: ASPECT of LIFE***
OH! THIS HANDKERCHIEF . . .

Oh! This pretty, laced, piece of fabric, called a 'handkerchief', it's utility 'par excellence' despite its micro size. It ungrudgingly lends a helping hand, to soak our tears, tears of happiness or sorrow, spreading out like a shell, to hold the pearls. A beloved's token of love, left unknowingly at her lover's threshold, when she runs away shyly as the clock strikes twelve and soon it becomes the lover's prized possession. A waving sign of affection, as the royalty passes by, the enthusiasm so vibrant in its happy jerks. A casket for the multitude of fragrances, each fold smiling with the fragrance of the perfumes of Arabia. Always resplendent with designs, ever so dainty, a pink flower peeping from one of its corners, or a cluster of red cherries. A phenomenon of pastel colours in their variant hues, so soothing to the eyes, adding colour as and when. Gifted with affection to friends and relatives, breathing in the drawers, a memory of that precious moment. This 'handkerchief' a lady's and a gentleman's best friend, till the end.

112: ASPECT of LIFE***THE GUESS GAME

Life is a 'guess game', from the time you open your eyes, till the time you close them. Uncertainty in momentum, is the pendulum of life, question marks all the way are the landmarks of life's journey. "Is the baby going to be a girl or a boy?", "Will I get this job or not?", "Will tomorrow be as lovely as today?" Questions and questions keep clouding your mind, making you go berserk at times and to many an immediate answer hardly ever follows.

Answers are bound to time and it's only when time gives the 'green signal' that answers see the light of day, hidden in oblivion till then. You can't be sure of the next second, what talk of the next minute or tomorrow. As humans it becomes our forte to keep building grandiose plans, deluding ourselves into believing that we are the artisans of our lives, little realising that life unfolds each page according to the plan He has laid for us and He keeps you in the 'guess mode' till the last breath.

Has anyone been able to guess when he or she will close his or her eyes forever? Has anyone been able to guess as to what came first, the 'egg' or the 'chicken'? The 'guess game' goes on, keeping us 'guessing' at every step.

113: ASPECT of LIFE***HAPPINESS

'Happiness' is a very relative term, what maybe happiness for me, may not be for another. It has several offshoots and each offshoot reaches out to different people at different times. How best it is put to use is a test of our wisdom. For some simply 'daydreaming' with the feet up, gives a kick which nothing else can. For the 'nosey people' stalking people, like a shadow from their first till their last breath, gives them a remarkable source of sustenance. Then we have the 'gossip mongers', who make their 'bellies laugh' at the cost of others. The so called 'pious' people who spend hours begging God for His mercy, and it takes them little to be merciless towards others, a sadistic happiness. A 'painter, a writer, a poet' who gets lost to the world, in the pursuit of their ideas, spilling them out, as though straight from the heart. Men who spend the better part of their lives, eyeing the wives of others, as though there can be no better food for the eyes. 'Partying', with those hollow, plastic smiles, are for some, precious moments spent on trivialities, as though, nothing can be better.

What we forget in our 'quest for happiness' is the quality of the 'happiness' we are hankering for . . . is that much sought after 'happiness' as glistening and short lived like the dew drops . . . or as glistening and eternal as the stars?

114: ASPECT of LIFE***TRINITY

'Trinity forms the footstool of our lives, the past, present and the future'. Neither can be de-linked from the other, flows into the other, like the three tributaries of the same river, the river of life. The experiences of the past, the joys and the sorrows, become the touchstones for our breaths of the present.

We learn from our past mistakes, becoming the wiser for it and are able to discriminate between what will be good and bad for us, the past standing as our 'guardian angel'. The present is the main focus, to 'live in the present' is what the old sages go by. Take each day as it comes by, living each moment to the fullest, making every moment a landmark for the future. The future is a curtain which lies ahead of us, revealing itself just as much, as and when. It's a ticklish situation, the past gliding into the present and the present gliding into the future, as though holding each other's hand, doing a rock-n-roll, to the sound of human laughter.

115: ASPECT of LIFE***
THE GOSSIP MONGERS

The 'gossip mongers', a class in themselves, a set of people I keep miles away from. Still they can sniff you out, their power of smell so potent, as to put a 'sniffer dog' to shame. Their calling is to sniff at, and then bring out their 'sniffer package' into the glare of public light, with of course a good deal of peppering here and there. The 'grapevine' grows best in their gardens and why not, doesn't it get just the right manure to thrive at its best. The uncanny knack of discovering 'skeletons in the cupboard' is God's gift to them, skeletons of which you may have not the vaguest idea. Stocked with all the, so-called valuable sniffings, their job of tearing the person's reputation swings into action with full force and by the time their session is over, their victim is left with a threadbare semblance of the clothing he was in and the best part is, it's all done in absentia of their victim, the poor victim innocently ignorant of the mass scale massacre.

Everyone's business is theirs, but their own . . . and so professional are they, if they happen to bump into you . . . a sweeter smile and a warmer bear hug, can never be . . . the 'tatters' are craftily hung on your back. The 'gossip mongers' lives are lives, indeed well spent . . . sniffing and barking . . . at all and sundry . . . a life 'well spent' . . . at the 'cost of others'.

116: ME***MY MUMMY IS FOREVER

That day still looms large in my life, how could that day have taken away my mother who was, to me, a 'Mummy forever'? The numbness, the denial, the shattering thought, that the word 'forever' had gone into oblivion, in that moment when my mother breathed her last and then that excruciating pain, a pain which ripped me apart, at the realisation.

An epitome of all that goes into that one word 'Mummy', always so loving, so giving, never complaining and never expecting. Twenty-two long years, without my father, still with what exclusive grace and dignity she had conducted herself, managing beautifully within the resources left to her by my father, living each day, the way my father would have liked her to, doing him proud at every moment. Endowed with a beauty, which made her stand apart in a crowd, her mannerisms as becoming in their modesty. As I sat alone in her room, lost in my thoughts, I broke into tears like never before, craving for her arms around me, just one more time. It was as though I felt her gentle, loving hands wipe away my tears, those tender hands which had always held mine, guiding me, propelling me, as and when and the sudden awakening that, 'my Mummy is forever'. Her gentle love, her giving always with a smile, the happiness, she spread around, living each day to the fullest, were her legacy to her children. A legacy of a 'Mummy', who will always live with me, every second, every minute, of my life . . . 'forever'.

117: ME***THE ABSENCE—OR IS IT?

The one and only truth of life . . . death . . . we all shy away from . . . but it knocks at everyone's door, sooner or later. Her father's ever so sudden farewell to her, twenty-three years back, had hit her like a tornado. More so because of her intense attachment and blind dependence on him, despite her marriage old by fourteen years. She could vividly recall its shattering effect, the first three months. Gradually and very gradually she started coming to terms with his absence from her life forever but was he really gone?

She could still feel his boundless love for her, a love which kept giving her the strength to move on. Never the one to sit and educate her about life, he simply let the education drop by mannerisms solely his and this education became the guidelines of her life. It was as though pages after pages started opening up from her book, pages she had not been aware of till now. A page which made her smile with love . . . a page which made her cry in remembrance . . . a page which gave her the strength to move on . . . but always with her father by her side . . . and she took each step fearlessly . . . with her head held high . . . doing her father proud at every step.

118: ASPECT of LIFE***TIME

Someone once happened to mention, 'Time is static'. I pondered and realised how true the words are. Time is static because it's always in momentum, it never stops. Keeps moving at the cost of everything, from our first till our last breath, never taking a breather. A mute spectator of our joys and sorrows, unaffected, also the biggest healer, in its own detached way. Capricious to the hilt and we, helpless victims in its hands, laughing and crying, as and when. Time is beyond time, always 'sweet sixteen'. It ticks by, never a second less and never a second more, each second ticked by is a present second gone into the past and the present second is a second which will take us into the future.

The needle of time always moves in a circle, forming a zero, depicting that life is but a zero and that everything goes full circle. So beware of time because though it is beyond our vision, it can be felt. A caress now and a blow next. Time needs to be respected, handled in just the right manner. At the end of the day, it's time alone which will stand testimony to our lives, to be remembered with love or to be just passed by.

119: ASPECT of LIFE***SELF-IMAGE

Simply masks and masks all around, a compulsive need to project an untarnished, image of ourselves, where little can be taken at face value. Promises are made to be broken . . . say something now and immediately turn a 'volte-face' . . . make excuses to save our skin . . . indulge in sycophancy to meet our ends . . . be 'sugar and honey' to the face and rip apart the person's reputation, the moment the back is turned . . . it's all so frightening. We spend our lives trying to fool others by our so called 'street smartness', doing everything possibly wrong to project that perfect public image. Is it really worth all the effort that goes into it? Little do we realise, we can fool the world, but we can't fool ourselves. A mask will ever remain a mask, hiding our true selves because we have lots to hide and we hide what we are afraid to project. So a lifetime goes in 'hiding' and 'projecting'.

None of us have the time to reflect on that 'day' when each one of us will be compelled to stand in front of our mirror, in all our nakedness. Stripped of our so-called masks, a big question mark against our 'bona fides' and will feel deprived of that simple freedom of seeing our own reflection in the mirror because a mirror projects only the truth.

120: ASPECT of LIFE***MATCH FIXING

The match-fixing was depicted, though in an exaggerated manner, best by the Bollywood movies of the sixties. The boy's family smugly sitting in the sitting room while the girl's family, all jittery, hovers around. Obviously with their heart's in their mouths, apprehensive of how their daughter will be liked by the suitor and his family. In walks the girl, all dolled up like a doll from a shop shelf, with a tray in her hands, the laden tea cups clattering against one another, like the bones in her body, so nervous is she. Half the cups drop on the floor as she tries to put them on the table. The boy either leers at the girl or gets up and strides off in a huff, with his family in tow and the girl's family in tears. The reel unfolds further.

How far have we gone since then? Miles, step by step. A little modernity came our way with the girl and the boy allowed to take some time out, alone at the rendezvous, while their parents indulged in the give and take handshakes or built mountains of praises of their respective babies. In a matter of half an hour of a coochie-coo betwixt the pair, their destiny is decided for the better or the worse, as they return to the respective laps of their parents with a smile or a scowl.

The sun shone a little brighter and after the meeting, long tete-e-tetes started over the cell or the exchange of mails, with the end of the line, either tying the nuptial knot or making each go in the opposite direction, never wanting to see the other's face again.

Of course the moon now lends it's rays, flooding the bedroom, as the girl and the boy share the bed, before reaching the altar. The much popular live-in relationship, whereby the bride loses her virginity to a boy, who may or may not decide to marry her and vice-versa. It matters tuppence though, for another bed is waiting, just round the corner, to be slept in and shared for eternity or not.

All the exuberance and the awaiting pleasure of the first wedding night has become a tale of the past, what with each knowing the other, inside out. A virgin girl or a virgin boy is looked upon as a freak by their peers. The clattering of the cups, the coyness, the virgin feel, the awakening of each other towards one another, has as though become a tale of yore, best forgotten as a twinkling star behind the unpredictable clouds.

121: ME***LEGACY OF WISDOM

I can vividly recall that evening, some years back, when my elder son was to step out on his own into the world, having completed his engineering. I heard a voice as though whispering to me "Mummy, the time has now come to impart your last legacy of wisdom to your son." That afternoon I told Chugoo, "I want to speak to you today. My words, I hope will stand you in good stead in your future life."

In the early hours of the evening, Chugoo sat across from me on the dining table and I handed over to him a package, a priceless package, no amount of wealth or position can give. A package I had come by, by my every breath of life, happily or unhappily, vide experiences, good or bad but nevertheless a wholesome education, which no amount of literacy can impart.

"Chugoo, tomorrow you will be leaving to be on your own in this world. We, as always will be there for you but it's not going to be the same, since it is you who will be facing every minute of your life to the best of your ability. I as a mother, have tried more than my level best to bring you up, wrapped up in the value system as I deemed fit, within the confines and limitations of the family's scenario." (I was living with my in-laws.) Tears welled up in my eyes as Chugoo extended his arms to hold mine. That clasp with it's quiet warmth and understanding of my son towards my tribulations as though washed them all away.

I moved on "Chugoo in life, will you always find a path which at some juncture will bifurcate. One path will be the easier one, yielding quicker results, with you compromising with your values at every step. Remember each compromise will make easier the next one, till values will stop to hold any meaning. At the end of the path, will you be a winner or a loser, your conscience will alone tell you so, leave alone the world, it matters not. You will have fallen in your eyes with no respect worth the dime left for yourself."

"The other path will be the difficult one, by which you will endeavour to take each step, keeping your values and upbringing as stepping stones. Temptation will rear it's head many a times but sidetracking it, will you move on. At the end you will get the most prized gift, of being proud of the integrity of your character, of being proud of yourself, in totality."

I stopped then, as a choke filled my throat and then carried on "Your Amma decided to take her first step on the second path, tough, nonetheless, and am I not a proud Mommy today, when I see both my sons proud of me? It's now for you to decide to go the way your Amma went or otherwise."

Though I sent him the next day with a brave face and all my blessings, I cried oceans after he left, till there were no tears left to be wiped away. It's been now, nearly 13 years since my little bird flew out of the nest to fend for himself. Am I not the blessed mother of a son, who decided upon the path his Amma had stepped on, three and a half decades back?

122: ME***THE WOMEN OF BIHAR

This write up on the women of Bihar, is based entirely on my assessment of them, as I have perceived them to be, during my stay here for the last three decades and a half. Hopefully it will be a fair, balanced approach, bringing to light their strengths and weaknesses. There may be some amongst my limited readers who may fall out with my opinion, my only request to them is to "Please close your eyes, take in a deep breath and then let what I have written sink in. I'm sure the rancour will evaporate amidst it's fumes."

The women of Bihar are undoubtedly blessed with a lot many qualities, which I find to be lacking in women generally. They happen to be extremely practical and focused and can work really hard to achieve their end. Their power of resilience is remarkably elastic helping them to make the best of whatever they have and adjusting anywhere to the best of their ability. Most can actually rough it out and still have the remnants of energy to socialise and entertain. Genetically blessed, with all the knack of keeping their husbands well, by this I mean really well, within their regimental control and for any woman, believe me it's an asset worth laurels. Those who are, are extremely methodical and organised and it can be vice-versa as well, to the same degree. They happen to be well turned out, taking pains to match their clothing to the best of their ability. A great deal is made easy for them in life because their husbands have no option left but to toe their line.

On the other hand they are generally endowed with a good deal of craftiness, cleverness and can turn volte-face at the blink of an eye. Lack the softness at heart and can be emotionally tough to a degree, which goes beyond my imagination. As I have mentioned, their husbands dare not go against their wishes or else their lives can be made miserable to an extent, that they much succumb than be made a victim of their modus-operandi. To be honest the men of Bihar are best handled and managed by the women of Bihar. Their dress sense verges a little on the crude side, that style with a finesse is somewhat lacking. Of course, those who have had the benefit of external exposure are much better turned out. Like everywhere else there

173

are families with the women somewhat poised but the fundamental nature remains the same.

Like in every other state the women of Bihar are endowed with their plus and minus, as I have perceived them to be and wanted to share the same, exceptions are always there, as everywhere. Have endeavoured my best to be pragmatic and unbiased. Speaking for myself, though my husband belongs very much to Bihar I can never mould myself to the basic nature of the women here since it's so diagonally opposite to mine. My small, little niche is good enough for me, for as I am, good or bad, liked or unliked.

123: ME***LOVE AND PASSION

Apart from writing which is my love and passion my other interests lie in painting and bird watching. Of course catching butterflies and playing pranks or throwing tantrums were my love and passion as a child, which have now gone into the haze of clouds, though the memories remain ever as vivid.

As painting goes, my imagination when it comes to creating something on my own is pretty vacant but, yes, I can copy a painting to perfection. I remember my mother taking a monthly magazine called *Woman and Home*. There used to be a story in it which would always have an attractive illustration of a woman's face and I would sketch it with a pencil with my father as my critic. "The eyes haven't got that expression" . . ."The nose is a little long". These small corrections paved the way to my minutest of minute observations when in the process of copying one such. A pencil sketch of a girl's profile with a pensive look still adorns our bedroom wall till today.

I like bird watching and look longingly at their freedom as they do flit from one place to another. What bliss! Always busy with their harmless pursuits, their camaraderie par excellence. Let a baby crow drop from the nest and a flock of crows will assemble from nowhere in no time, ready with their beaks to hit anyone who dare ventures near, their cacophony drowning the entire neighbourhood. The birds, always in pairs, helping each other, with no ego hassles. Different flights, some jerky, some smooth, some graceful. Their varied shapes and colours so eye-catching, their small mannerisms holding me spellbound for hours.

Each with their own love and passions, so long it gives you the happiness you are looking for, if not forever at least for the time you are engrossed in it.

124: ASPECT of LIFE***SILENCE

It always feels kind of strange when I resume my writings after a hiatus. The last 17 days whence I had gone into a sort of self-imposed silence was not without ample reason. I wanted to deduce the 'power or silence'. My mind kept jostling with the gamut of thoughts, as did my fingers ache to pour it all down onto my iPad and it sure took some effort to hold myself from doing so.

Anyway it was indeed a restraint well done. For one I have become a little more wise regarding the ways of this world. All that had come to stay in me have taken deeper roots. If one fish stops coming to the water surface to take a breather, it's not as if the other fish' die or the beauty of the ocean gets any the less. The water life carries on as though nothing has happened. It's great while you are there and equally great if you are not there. I'm a fountain of bubbling emotions and it's time I learnt to reserve them for those whom I love and care for and vice-versa. Easier said than done, for me though . . .

Life is an encyclopaedic study of sorts. Any unhappy, deep realisation is followed by a good deal of pain and anger but the realisation is worth the turmoil. You get deeper and deeper enmeshed with the ground realities which otherwise seldom come to the forefront on their own. No sapling blossoms into a tree with it's foliage and flowers without making the effort of planting and watering it.

So does life move on, an education at every step, hopefully making a wiser you before you take the next step. Silence can be very potent, if not for others, at least for yourself.

125: ME***THANK YOU PAPA

This goes back to the day of my wedding, whence the next day I went to the hotel where the groom and his family members were staying. My husband's grandfather 'Baba', for whom I carry a lot of deep regard always was also there. (Ours was the last wedding in the family which he attended.) After having sought his blessings he had looked at me and had said "You are the most beautiful and the only Post Graduate daughter-in-law amongst all the others who have come into my family." This compliment coming from Baba I treasure to this day.

Officially I was not a Post Graduate at the time of my wedding. There were two months to go for my finals. Hence after my '*Rukhsati*' I went to Tilouthu, my husband's home village and returned to Lucknow straight from there to appear for my pending exams.

Now started my tantrums, since I was absolutely in no mood to study, more so since studies had never been my sweetheart and my wedding gave me a good excuse for not appearing for the exams. Every day the usual "I will not, I will take the exams the next year" . . . and my Papa's "Oh! Yes you will, this year itself, even if you fail." This tug of war would begin at the breakfast table to get stalled at dinner time, at least for the time being, with the withered rope crying for mercy.

Eventually one day Papa made a statement which somehow wriggled it's way to my good sense. "You will ever remain a Graduate for life, by not appearing for your finals now. Two years of hard work will get flushed down the drains because of these couple of months before your finals." This sentence of his convinced me with it's logic and, heartbroken, I once again put my sniffling nose to my voluminous books. Pushing my daydreams into the backyard, I started attending classes in the University, so as not to fall short of attendance. Appeared for the papers and then waited for the viva-voce, which was to take place a fortnight later.

I came to Bokaro, where my husband is an entrepreneur and was in a joint business with his father, three months after my marriage. The results came out while I was here, missing my first division by a couple of percentage. At least I had not plugged as was my apprehension. Baba's words didn't go waste and neither did my father's. Had I not appeared for my exams then, I would ever have remained a Graduate, for the real exams of life began soon after. Where would I have had the peace and the energy to appear for my exams the following year? Thank you Papa, for all your love and wisdom.

126: ASPECT of LIFE***CAKE-WALK?

Life is not a cake-walk. There's a lot in life to laugh over, to cry over and to laugh and cry over both. The ratio of course varies from one person to the other, as do the issues. If life was not a pull of opposites perhaps Newton would never have landed on the 'Law of Gravity'.

It is this subtle and sometimes obvious blend of the joys and sorrows, which give us a taste of their real feel. When in the throes of happiness do we realise the essence of happiness and so with sorrow. Like everything temporal they are transient and fleeting. Try locking them up in a casket and will you be bewildered by their sheer capriciousness.

To talk of reaching a state of mind where you remain unaffected by either is again verging on the idealistic, which I feel is not practical at all. It's not that there are not people who have been able to exercise that control over the mind but how many? Perhaps one in a million. A mind boggling ratio.

The most grounded way of being happiness and sorrow savvy, so to say, is to give each their required space and time. Not to start scaling the clouds nor to start cursing your fate. Enjoy every moment of the radiance, drinking it to the lees and when the blues hit, cry your heart and soul out like never before. Remembering always, every night sees a morning and every morning sees a night. However never let them get the better of you, to be at their mercy, for then will you feel the falling from the clouds with a hurtling impact.

Yes, life indeed is not a cake-walk but can leave imprints of the feet for others to follow. All the creamy footprints which will yell, how wondrously and beautifully have you managed to keep the cake intact despite having cut it into pieces or "You can have your cake and eat it too", in this context. Per se, making do with the plethora of happiness and sorrow at the same wavelength.

127: ME***MY WRITINGS?

There are many times I question myself as to what am I doing to extend a hand towards those who need support and help? Is penning down my emotions or expressing my views on various aspects enough? Will mere written words find a solution to their problems? No, if viewed dispassionately. Then what am I doing?

Am I simply writing on umpteen linings of life, expressing my concern related to them or relating my varied experiences and the nostalgic feels? A mode of catharsis, a love and passion getting released. Yet yes, there is something much beyond.

Sharing vide whichever means is an art very few are endowed with. By this I mean not just sharing, I mean sharing with an absolutely open heart and transparency. Thoughts, feelings and emotions which pass on through my pen as though through a clean duct attached to my heart. For then I stand not challenged in my own eyes, leave alone the world. Some may find something worthwhile in my sharings to dwell upon. There are those amongst my readers for whom my write ups maybe a stress-buster or simply a pleasurable past-time. A smile on their faces will be akin to a smile on mine.

My views are entirely mine, may or may not be agreed with by others. We all have our own manner of viewing life but at least my angle gets afloat in the open air, and one never knows when a certain spike may open new vistas for someone.

I do extend a helping hand in whatever manner I deem best towards those who need to be helped and are comfortable accepting it so. One of my deepest urge is to do whatever best I can, in as subtle a manner as I can, to be anonymous as much as I can and to never expect anything in return.

Perhaps these are the small nondescript attachments of my writings. If even one reader gets to benefit from them, in a manner whichever, it's a passion well agreed with by me.

128: ME***IN QUANTUM MOTION

There is no delete button which can make you do away with your destiny in the hopes of creating a new one, as per your likes and fancies. Yes, you can't delete your destiny but you can manage your destiny. How well or badly depends on your calibre to do so.

I can speak for myself and my journey, as it went, in this regard. Of course, the word destiny came into play in my life after I got married and gradually it gained ground. Extremely naive and gullible that I was in the ways of the world, having had an extremely protected upbringing, I was like hauled against a tornado, to survive or to die.

Not at all religious by nature, since I had not seen any kind of a religious sham at my parent's place but seeing my mother-in-law pray for long hours (and being none the better for it) brought me into the traps of rituals and a binding routine. The fear of all the tribulations in my life made me an easy prey. Added to this, my father who stood like a rock for me, his demise barely after 13 years of my turbulent marriage, made my insecurities further magnified. I found myself buckling at the knees and the more I buckled, the more my blind faith in all the religious beliefs sucked me in, like quicksand. The wavering hopeless hope of seeing everything set right in my life, if I kept bending my knees in front of those statues. With me losing my self-confidence at every step and those hollow rituals, supposedly changing my destiny for the better.

Questions and counter questions, with their ever open questions marks, started to make their rounds in my mind, bogging me down endlessly, till one fine day, I simply made a clean break from all these strangulating ropes which I had tied around my neck. I felt literally like a free bird, which had suddenly grown wings and was going to fly on the strength of it's own wings, taking the right directions, even when flying against the wind.

I stand on my own two feet today, managing my destiny to the best of my ability with the mental and emotional resources of mine at hand. The unbending belief, of every minute taking it's course at the hands of destiny forms the backdrop of my life. How best I can manage this destiny for my happiness, is well within my hands.

My life rests at the feet of my 'Lord' with no prayers or rituals to bind me with, for I connect with Him through my love and unyielding faith. A free bird am I today, which has learnt through trial and error the gracefulness of the flight, with the wings in quantum motion.

129: ME***THE MOON

In my childhood the moon was riddled with stories and poems, as did I listen to them with big, open eyes and my mouth agape. That shadow on the moon was that of an old woman spinning a wheel, sitting comfortably on the moon. Drawing pictures of the moon like a human face, looking so cute with it's eyes, nose and the warm smile. The magical, silver ball beaming up in the sky, playing hide and seek with the clouds, never did lose it's charisma.

Came teens and the moon glided from it's kiddish magic into the magic of romance. That silver, translucent glow adding warmth to the hugs and kisses of the lovers, as their loving, caressing whispers travelled to it's soothing glow. The lover promising to get anything in the world for his beloved and she cheekily asking for the moon, as her beauty was compared in hyperboles by the lover. The rays of the moon flowing in through the laced curtains in my bedroom, adding miles to my imagination and that wistful smile playing on my lips. Life was indeed blessed and as romantic as the moon up there.

Into adulthood and the moon started slipping into the clouds to make it's presence felt only on those few moments when life set apart it's blinds, for a wanting moment. The privacy it had basked in was trespassed by astronauts landing on the moon, throwing it's mystic touch to the winds. The scientific realisations of it's effect on human life and the earth further drew it's charm behind the curtains as did the awareness of the mythological beliefs.

Where did disappear the magical ball amidst the clouds? Of course it's right there, promising it's presence, unfailingly, day in and day out. Come hail, come storm but as you look up it's beaming presence never fails to bring a smile. Though umpteen years have flown by, yet never has it betrayed it's unyielding support to me. A support so huge, for when I find myself in the blues I just have to look up at the moon in the sky and get lost in it's cool yet warm glow, the poems and the stories of yore, playing "Ringa-ringa roses . . ." with my ever vivid imagination as I do flit away on my imaginary wings into the welcoming arms of the moon.

VANDANA SINHA

130: ME***MIDSUMMER NIGHT

"I know a bank where the wild thyme blows,
Where ox-lips and the nodding violet grows,
Quite over canopied with luscious woodbine,
With sweet musk roses and with eglantine."
These lines from Shakespeare's *Midsummer Night's Dream* ring a bell, as
tonight is the Midsummer Night bringing to mind this play and did I get
goose-bumps as I was penning these lines said by Oberon, reminding me of
my English Literature classes.

The Midsummer Night is as important a festival in most of the
European countries, as Christmas or the New Year and celebrated with as
much fanfare and mythological beliefs.

It is generally believed that fairies and elves visit the earth on the
Midsummer Night and have a festive time. A general belief also is of the
souls leaving the human body that night for a sojourn of the aerial regions.
Fires are lighted on the hills and as the hills become aflame the celebrations
crack with mirth and good hopes for the future.

As for me I will sit lost in my thoughts in the garden, with a candle
lighted and a spray of flowers in a dainty Belgian cut glass vase decorating
the table. My heart will be desperate to lay my eyes on a fairy or an elf
prancing around, even if for a fleeting moment or to be borne in the arms
of a fairy amidst the clouds but I know as always, it will be merely wishful
thinking. Then late in the night will I go to sleep with 7 flowers kept under
my pillow, for good luck.

Still I will have paid my respects with heartfelt warmth to this
Midsummer Night, as my spirit will revel in the soothing glow of the
candle flame, with my senses seeped in the mild fragrance of the flowers, my
innocent imagination playing with the innocence of the fairies and the elves.

131: ME***A TAIL?

The British left our country in 1947, giving us our much fought for freedom but have surely left their tail behind and a pretty long one at that. Many are there who are wanton to the British ways and to be honest I'm also one amongst them. I certainly am not proud to announce as much but what is, is and I'm not ashamed to write so. How can I deny a fact of which I find myself a victim?

I like things with an English touch because it's deep down there in me. In fact to think otherwise will be simply going against my innate character. My familiarity with the English language, English Literature, my choice of belongings, my mannerisms, my temperament, my penchant for a cosy, quaint, little cottage and what have you for asking are very English. Yes the only way in which I differ is my value system which is truly Indian, without any regrets. I am made that way and I have never struggled to be other than what I am.

Perhaps it's in my genes. My grandfather was extremely British in his lifestyle, with a butler to serve his meals catering to courses on an immaculately, well laid table. He hosted banquets but was a teetotaller himself. I have heard from my father how magnetic a presence he was blessed with. Over six feet tall and handsome in his British suits, his stepping in would make heads turn. Never of course did he give way to the British, merely because he happened to be an English person. Held on to his stand whenever he had to and held an extremely respectable place amongst the people including the English. I happen to be his granddaughter and have probably got it all from him and my father, who was, if not British in his lifestyle but certainly very British in his mannerisms.

To say, I ape the British will be putting it wrongly. It's as though it's all a part and parcel of me. The British undoubtedly have left and gone, more than half a century back but have left huge traces behind, of which I am a living example. I don't feel proud to announce so but am honest to accept so.

132: ME***BED OF ROSES

Today I smile a smile of wisdom as I remember an exchange betwixt my aunt (My mother's younger sister) and me on the eve of my wedding. She had asked me "Vandana, what is your concept of marriage?" Without so much as an in-between pause had I replied "Marriage to me is being in a cosy, little cottage with pretty floral curtains flying in the breeze and a bottle of Coke by my bed side." She had smiled and said "Remember Vandana, marriage is not a bed of roses."

Scant attention had I paid to her golden words then. To be honest I had not even allowed those words to sink in, so wrapped up was I in my sweet, little, hunky-dory world of blooming roses, of course sans the thorns. How I had shrieked and howled, literally pulling the roof down, when one such had pricked my finger as a child.

Soon all the fanfare of my marriage the next day and me as though a property of another family, in a matter of hours. The family in whose boundless love and care I had budded and blossomed, as if having lost its complete hold over me. Little had I fathomed then, how the first, the best and the loveliest chapter of my life had shut it's doors on my face forever. Little did I know then, of life's manifold chapters which would open and close without forewarnings. Each chapter an education, an awakening of sorts and me henceforth alone, scuffling and still holding on with all my might, crumbling and heaving myself up, again and again, to the gradual but strong realisation of those words "Remember Vandana, marriage is not a bed of roses."

The dreamy cottage with the wicker gate opening onto to a flowering lawn, the floral curtains swaying in the breeze, pampering my bottle of Coke, was but a figment of my vivid and naive imagination, to be blown away as swiftly with the breeze. As was I soon to learn with a heavy heart, marriage is certainly not a 'bed of roses' or so to say if it is a 'bed of roses' it's certainly not bereft of thorns.

RANDOM THOUGHTS

133: ME***CHOOSY

I have always been choosy about my friends. In school also I never moved around with the gang but had a limited number of friends, of course with whom there were no barriers in between. So also till today. Few but very dependable people whom I allow to come close to me. With everyone else it's a casual acquaintanceship, never a friendship.

My friendship is never ever measured by material well-being parameters. It bounces automatically on the person as a person. Genuineness, warmth, honesty, simplicity, values are the very simple traits which endear me. Very simple but so hard to come by in today's world, yet I do come by.

My hunches work manifolds regarding my friendships and they have never failed me or given me cause for regret. On f/b off and on I get requests from strangers which I look past or when online a 'Hi' from somebody in my message box, whom I don't know from Adam, which is again ignored. However there was a friend request which I got from a Swedish lady and without so much as a second thought I accepted. There is so much I'm trying to imbibe from her to make myself a better me. I am not only exceedingly fond of her but hold a lot of regard for her as well. So my hunch once again smiled at me. Being a spontaneous person I get these hunches like lightning and instantly the decision is made.

My choosiness is not only limited to friends but treads on every aspect of my life, once again devoid of preferences by way of money. Whatever it be has to simply say a big, big warm, sincere "Hello" and there it's within the circle of my arms.

VANDANA SINHA

134: ASPECT of LIFE***HATS

This hat has it's own distinctive place in the gallery of accessories, with stories hidden betwixt it's seams. A gentleman's and a gentle lady's dignified adornment which has always roused my interest and respect.

I remember the hat stand kept in the veranda of my house in Lucknow. So elegant in it's mahogany wood with the shining brass pegs. I had often wondered as to the various hats of the various people it must have been a temporary custodian of during my grandfather's days. There are so many pictures of his, mostly with a Bowler hat on.

There are as many types of hats for ladies and men as there are different types of heads which it so artfully covers giving just the required amount of leverage. Go to a hat section in a store and the eyes literally pop out at the sight of the shapes, colours and their names. Different hats for different occasions, well adapted. They too have their own protocol to follow and to be followed to perfection, the donners equally fastidious about the norms.

The mannerisms attached to these hats are as endearing and of course a person who takes pleasure in wearing a hat has to be well versed with them or it'll be a real sham. The chivalrous, just that bit of tipping when greeting a lady. The flamboyant flourish with which it is removed for just as much time when wooing a charming one such. The taking it off at a solemn occasion as a mark of reverence. The careful carelessness in holding it when in a tete-e-tete with a friend. The ladies looking up coyly from behind the short laced veil attached to some. The dainty flowers and attachments to the ladies hats making them appear even the more enticing. Both the men and the ladies turning out for the better with their hats. At many a public place the hat is sent around to collect alms for charity. Can anyone refuse it so?

A small, little adornment like a hat, new or tattered, adding volumes to the personality of a gentleman and a gentle lady. This hat with it's own little world of names and tippings.

135: ME***ICE SALT

It's once again an evening of "Ummmm mmmmmmmmmmmmmmmmmmmmmmmmmmmmmmmmmmmm . . ." My mind has frozen once again. This time it seems like it's not the ice which can be removed with a shovel, it needs salt to melt it. Hope the salt will do it's required stuff.

Ya! My autograph book, which still holds it's prized place in my drawer in the chest of drawers in Lucknow. A pretty small autograph book with a floral cover and pages in all different colours. Oh! I can remember what a craze it was to take autographs from the family and friends and the enthusiasm coupled with curiosity which went into quickly going through the text.

My first page was of course autographed by whom, you guessed right, my Papa. I remember every word of it . . ." To my dearest Bindiya, Cleanliness is next to Godliness, From your dearest Papa" and well this penchant for cleanliness sticks like glue to me, to this day. Half my energy goes into keeping an immaculately, clean house. Now am I digressing? Let me. Sometimes that's the fun of writing, from one mountain peak to another. The second page, autographed by my Mummy . . ." My dearest Bindiya, Let your heart be as pure as the water of a brook, Your dearest Mummy". The other pages are all filled with autographs from my siblings, aunts, uncles, cousins and friends.

Must relate this one. Mr Saleem Durrani, the seasoned and handsome cricketer had come to Lucknow and was invited for dinner at my Uncle's place. We were also amongst the invitees and I in my frilly frock with the can-can, ballerina shoes and of course that cheeky grin of mine, walked up to Mr Durrani and requested him for his autograph. Was I holding onto the moon when he wrote after asking my name "To my sweet Vandana. With love, Saleem Durrani." How I preened and showed it off to everyone at home and school. Those small, little pleasures of life which were like a treasure for me then and continue to be so even now, need no casket but a simple, loving heart.

The salt has more than done it's job, hasn't it? See how I have flicked through the pages of my autograph book and still find myself clutching it to my bosom with all my love.

136: ASPECT of LIFE***
PUT ASIDE EVERYTHING

In the twilight the mourners stood around the coffin in the graveyard as the Pastor spoke those words which comprised the only though abject truth of life ". . . from dust unto dust . . ." and the coffin was lowered into the grave. The remains of the beautiful mother as prettily encased in her once bridal dress. A whole history, as though was going to be buried along with, though some chapters had died a natural death when she did breathe her last, as virgin like, cocooned in that cocoon of her memories, their purity never to be defiled by the touch of any other.

Her husband wiped the tears in the privacy of his room, never to be able to forgive himself for not taking the first flight back, as soon as he had got news of her sudden illness. At least in those last, parting moments he would have been able to hold her seeking hands, with that reassuring clasp, making all the difference to his wife, as did she lay, with her eyes fixed at the door, for a sight of his silhouette. He did take the first flight back as soon as he got that heart splitting news of her goodbye, but those seeking hands went without that reassuring clasp and neither did those seeking eyes have a glimpse of the silhouette.

The young, handsome son, the apple of his mother's eyes cursed himself for not having pushed aside everything, to be by his mother's side, when she needed him most. He turned the pages, never to find her wanting in his hour of need. His call always took dominance over her own. He cupped his chin in his hands and cried his heart out, as his mother's beautiful face stood smiling before him, as though telling him once again "I will hold your hand in one hand and your father's in the other, so will I breathe my last in the lap of my sweet, little family." Oh! And none was there to hold her simple wish because everything else took precedence over the most important.

This is the sad part. All of us do manage to show up, somehow and anyhow, when time and money become secondary but only after that person has left for the Heavenly abode. The importance of being with that person when your presence was being sought after by every receding breath somehow managed to escape notice because everything else was more important.

What is the use of shedding those tears now? Those tears which got locked in those eyes which closed forever will never spill now to get release. Those dreams which got shattered will never get fulfilled now, for those eyes have closed for eternity. Those relationships on whom rested the footstool of life, found everything more important than what was most important.

To put aside everything to be there by the person's side during those last moments and do whatever one can to give comfort and peace, is what is so needed. To do that little bit of putting aside everything else to be able to just hold the hand, and stamp the beauty of the relationship with that human touch, if nothing more.

137: ASPECT of LIFE***GREETINGS

There are innumerable countries over the world, with as many diverse cultures, individualistic in manner. Greeting others, a cultural aspect, has always held my interest. Somewhere I feel the mode of greeting reflects the warmth or the coldness of the people.

In India welcoming with a 'Namaste', said with both the hands folded is the traditional manner. Of course, the British have left but have left behind huge cultural chunks. Their greeting with a handshake is also much prevalent here.

In the U.S.A. the Americans are pretty easy going with their casual handshake and an equally casual 'Hello', bespeaking their not so stringent attitude towards life. The English are known for their rigidity in matters of etiquettes. A firm handshake betwixt men with a lighter touch betwixt a man and a woman, with a 'How do you do' is most common or simply the tipping of the hat, which speaks volumes with it's flamboyance and which I do find extremely fascinating. In the European countries double kissing is the accepted manner of welcoming a person, to be followed by a 'Good day' or a 'Good Evening', etc., as the case may be, in their national language. Like 'Bonjour' for a 'Good day' or 'Au revoir' for 'Good bye' in France. The Italians also greet with a double kiss and 'Ciao' or 'Salve' for 'Hello'. The Swedish are reserved and formal and prefer a handshake with a 'Hej' for 'Hello'. I can go on and on about the greetings endlessly, with the 'folding of hands' or a 'handshake' or a 'kiss'.

Come to think of it this small gesture is so very important. Not just carrying it out for the heck of it but the body language of the greeting is what matters. One can at once fathom the level of the welcoming breath and the following moments take their cue from there itself. I thank the stars though, in India 'a kiss' for a welcome has still to gain grounds, or else the sex starved men and women here will start greeting every second person on the road, under the pretext of greeting with a warmth which goes much beyond the normal. Thank the Lord for small mercies!

138: ME***FRIENDSHIP

Oh! To have an old friend visiting, is indeed a great feel, as I had mine over for the last couple of days. Became friends while she was here, many years back and shifted to Lucknow thereafter. Of course we always met during my trips to Lucknow but met her at my place for the first time ever since. A holiday at home.

Either time stood still or the 24 hours as though got compressed into a 1 blissful hour. Sharing our happiness and misgivings over the period of time. Tearing our husbands to shreds as we rattled off at breakneck speed about their uncountable shortcomings or strengths, the latter from their point of view, something we craved to do but never could to their faces, due to obvious reasons. Wow! One after another popping out like balloons. What fun. All their bravado and the bloated egos coming to naught.

Sharing our hopes and dreams, some having got fulfilled or perhaps others never to be. Baring our hearts out to each other like siblings without any reservations. Giving and seeking advice on matters innumerable. Many a times fathoming the other's thoughts even before they got spelled out, telepathy. Exchange of views on a wide range of subjects, sometimes verging on to the spiritual.

Nostalgic memories of our days spent here. Romping around like school girls or crying our hearts out till late in the evenings and then returning home with our laden hearts left behind into the depths of the evening shades. Lighter souls. Always there in each other's hour of need, with time never a constraint. Those moments when we had lent our shoulders for the other to cry upon, making our own shoulders the lighter. A catharsis of sorts.

Time came for her to leave as with moist eyes we hugged one another in the driveway, under the cloudy sky. The warm, pulsating bear-hug holding betwixt it's circle, years, the happiness and sorrows, the dreams and hopes, as of course the cribbings endless. An easiness and honesty, so hard to come by, a friendship which not only does justice to this small, little word but signifies in all sincerity, all that this word signifies.

139: ASPECT of LIFE***RACE

Race! Race! Race! Oh this Godammit race. Stand at the roadside and be a bewildered witness to the mad, rat race. My baffled mind simply watches and marvels at the hurry and the worry and asks "What is everyone running after?"

My mind each time asks the same question though it knows it'll come forth with the same answer. This maddening race is to grapple as much as one can of the material benefits which are ever so temporal. Of course amidst these frantic footsteps may be some also which are moving in a different direction altogether. For those for whom the purpose of life is to attain riches beyond these transient so-called.

No time for those special moments so rare, no time to sit and retrospect or introspect, no time to reach out, no time for anything to improve the quality of life. In the shortest possible time amass as much as you can, for you never know what will happen the next minute. So run as fast as your legs can take you.

Come to think of it our basic needs are the same, whether a pauper or a billionaire. The difference arises marking the status barriers when we start to quantify. A hut or a palatial mansion or mansions, a frugal meal or a seven course meal, tattered clothing or donning the best branded available, you walk to communicate or you mega drive to communicate, going for a holiday huddled in a bus or travelling in a chartered plane. Subsequently to be looked down upon or worshipped.

At the end of the day the requiem which sings "From dust unto dust" can be heard melting in the ears, as the coffin of a pauper or a billionaire is seen being lowered in the grave. Doesn't matter whether the coffin is worth tuppence or worth a million, a coffin remains a coffin.

The same manner of breathing, your first or your last, into this world. Leaving all that the race has dropped into your lap once you breathe your last, then why this mad, rat race? Taking things easy in the right manner will make life worth living, will add millions to your character, and will make you breathe your last with a wholesome breath.

140: ME***HOTCHPOTCH

Ummmmmmmmmmmmmmmmmmm mmmmmmm!

As I sit with my iPad open before me, there's really nothing in my mind to start coordinating my thoughts and my fingers with. A hopeless feeling, seems like I have penned on everything under the sky. Nothing seems to be left to be handled by my pen. What do I do now? Leave my ideas here or keep shaking my fingers on the key board, aimlessly. O.K. let's see what I eventually land up with? Probably this write-up is going to be a real hotchpotch of my thoughts.

Whenever I peep into my albums never do I find myself looking the same in any of the snaps. Slim and petite in one, weight gained in another, the ever young look in some and those crow feet in another, all poised and that carefree-carefulness in others, invariably different hair styles framing my face. A long, long history of my life compressed within the album pages, as do I get carried away to those bygone moments.

My wedding album which every time makes me wonder at my beauty. "Was I really that beautiful?" The captured beauty smiles back and says "Stupid you, if you were not, how come this snap?" Though I ought to thank the Lord for small mercies, for don't I make heads turn even today, despite the span of innumerable years. Oh! The narcissist that I am. My husband standing 10 inches over me, with me a Lilliputian beside him, merely 5 feet above sea level. So what!

The growing up years of my sons from toddlers . . . such cutie-pies, into teenagers . . . and now adults . . . strapping, handsome boys. Wonder how naturally I slipped into motherhood, a naive, pampered girl whose stepping out of teens was just a footstep away.

Seldom do I mull over the snaps of my parents for then do I start crying oceans. I do see the pictures but as quickly turn the pages, though that fleeting second never hesitates to make moist my eyes, nostalgic with the remembrance of their infinite love.

It's seldom, I get the time now to bury my nose betwixt the album pages but I know they are well within reach. Just reach out my arms and cuddle time as much as I wish to. This is where my thoughts have finally taken refuge today, the kaleidoscopic reel of my cinema.

141: ME***WHAT'S THERE IN A NICKNAME?

What is a name which substitutes the proper name of a person, a nickname of course and I love nicknames. Why? There is so much to them, isn't there? Absolutely loveable.

When you laugh or cry your first into this world, plonk, drops a nickname into your little lap. This sweet little name becomes your nickname, your unofficial, loving identity. This sweetness in most cases than not, hangs on till your last days, bringing in the flavour of the cradle innocence, whenever uttered. The proper, or may I say, the official name gets tagged later, becoming the identity of your image, your wealth, your position or whatever your so-called status be. The drooling naïveté takes the rear seat.

Inadvertently a nickname creeps up, spelling the characteristic which stands out best in a person, leaving you agape at the ingenuity. This of course refers to the nicknames which are given by friends or associates hitting at the most pronounced trait. When you hear somebody called by the nickname and though you may not have met the person, a caricature of one such will be there before you, not leaving you one iota surprised at the nomenclature when you do come face to face.

In every sphere of life do these nicknames mushroom. Be it home, school, workplace, in the starry world of love or in the world of enemies, will you find one stuck to your front or back. If the frontage comes into play, it's smiles and if the back-lot comes into play it's scowls. Either ways nicknames make their presence made felt with a heavy impact.

I find myself addressing everyone by his or her nickname, even when well aware of the proper name. Don't really know why. Perhaps have been attuned to it or feel more at home, doing so. I was and still am a great one at concocting nicknames but never ever with malice. My teachers in school were always the butt of it, specially my Hindi teacher. Used to call her "Eggy" because of the egg sized zeros she always complimented my Hindi marks with. Can I see that impish smile playing on my lips? Dear, wonder where she is now? I'm sure in her entire career she couldn't have got another student who maxed as much.

At home I was called "Bindiya" ever so lovingly by my parents, in school I was called "Vandy" and in the University "Snooty". Nicknames which have spanned years, lovingly called so, now lost in the misty haze with those who beckoned me with them. No, no, no, never can they be buried, when those who held my hands with those nicknames are always there with me, by my side. Can I hear my parents calling me with all their love "Bindiya"? Can I see that girl with the Chinese-cut fringe and the two pig-tails "Vandy" romping and giggling with her pals? Can I see that pretty, fair girl in the University, throwing her nose up in the air and walking away when seeing those gang of boys (all intellectuals, mind you) walking towards her to say "Hello"? Yes I can see that girl, though a woman now, still will these nicknames remain with me forever, memorable forever.

142: ASPECT of LIFE***NARCISSISM

I sure am a narcissist and mind you, a big, big one, like most of the people around. A human weakness or a human strength? Perhaps both, if viewed dispassionately because if I was not stricken with narcissism I wouldn't be what I am today. One of the many tucks of life which have made me what I am.

I look upon narcissism as a blessing to the extent, it proves how much I am in love with myself. Hence am I able to love others, of course, not on a general scale but only those whom I wish to love and well then, my love is as open as the sky above. Since I dote upon myself I do feel happy and flattered when this fancy of mine is reciprocated. Perhaps very few realise the importance of loving oneself. Those who don't, suffer from an immense feeling of degradation, which invariably leads towards a path strewn with hatred, envy, vengeance, discontentment and what have you. Making one feel and also come across as a despicable, unliked person, always down in the dumps.

Narcissism becomes a weakness when it oversteps it's bounds. I have very well assessed myself as a person or am well acquainted with myself and make no bones about it, to the extent if a situation so requires, I rattle off my weaknesses sooner than my strengths because I am not ashamed of them despite the former being as huge as the latter. Had I been blind and secretive of my weaknesses I wouldn't be as strong a person as I am today because I have nothing to hide. To be honest it's the lackings in me and my candid approach towards them, which add as though millions to my character. Also never do I take amiss if others point them out and why should I? What is, is, I don't deny it either but yes, if wrongly accused of a shortcoming, well then the person better be prepared for a tornado. My efforts at rectifying them continues though my eyes are open to the adage 'Old habits die hard'. Those who are not aware of their lackings or try to camouflage them, it's then that narcissism becomes a curse. They are the ones who are never able to grow and keep stagnating for life. Their strengths taking a back seat or always in the reverse gear.

Love me or hate me, will I continue to be a narcissist, hard to be reckoned with. My unmatched narcissism blessing me with the capacity to dote on those, whom I wish to dote upon and flying on the seventh cloud when my narcissism is so fanned.

143: ASPECT of LIFE***NAMELESS

Every relationship is defined with a name, duties and expectations which are attached to it, narrowing it's existence to the relationship as it be. However there are certain relationships which go beyond the limitations of any name, which cannot be tied down to any peg.

Such relationships are very rare and a blessing. Since they go beyond any kind of a nomenclature, their abandonment of freedom is unique in it's essence. The connect simply happens, as though out of the blue and builds up, brick by brick, creating a strong structure to be blindly relied upon. A stepping beyond the boundaries of duties and the resulting expectations. No wantings, still arms are extended to hold in times of dire need. Shoulders are given to lay your head upon when the heart is too heavy with pain. Happiness shared like the happiness is equally from both the ends. A trust in the confidence which no storm can shake, leave alone break. A blessing which is always there like your Guardian Angel ready to take you in it's arms, at the merest feel of need.

I treasure such a one for it overrides any man-made structure and is always so becoming. You have to experience it's beatific beauty and the abandonment to a get a real feel of it's tenderness and the depth of feelings like an awakening of sorts. An ethereal touch which goes beyond the horizon, spreading it's soothing aura of delight.

A relationship which just happens as though destiny deemed it so. The gay abundance of the shared laughter, tears and confidences never betrayed, a cooling sensation of belonging, in each other's company. A relationship with the wings of a bird, flying sky high, for the sky is the limit for one such, a relationship which smirks at the very thought of being constricted to a name.

144: ME***ALCOHOL

There was a time when I couldn't stand the sight of alcohol. The reason being perhaps it's taboo in my family. As I had mentioned earlier, my grandfather though extremely British in his ways, was a teetotaller and so also was my father and my five uncles, all of course living in the same house.

Being mulish right as a child, I was as mulish about the person I was to get married to, to be a teetotaller as well. When enquired by my father he was told as much and so heaving a sigh of relief I ventured into marriage. A couple of days after my wedding I retired to bed but my husband preferred to hang around with his cousins till late into the night. Very understandable but what was not understandable was, when I learnt from a cousin of his the very next morning, of the opening of a bottle of champagne that night to celebrate the arrival of a newly born of a cousin. With my heart beating loud did I ask her "Did my husband also have champagne?" I can still hear the thudding of my heartbeat when I had heard her answer "Yes", said so indifferently as though, what was the big deal. The first bombshell post marriage came hurtling, hitting me right in the face, little did I know then of the stack which lay ahead, mostly all in my mother's-in-law closet.

I would wince whenever I'd see my husband enjoying a drink with his cousins or friends, my chagrin crossing all bounds. Once after toasting at a friend's place, my temper got the better of me and I simply picked up my husband's glass and emptied it all in the flower bed nearby, though I had no business to do so, especially after a toast had been offered. His friend lost his temper, as did I, much to my husband's embarrassment. Who the Hell cared?

Gradually, though very gradually of course, I got used to seeing this grape decoction being enjoyed to the hilt and it doesn't rub me the wrong way now. I of course continue to be a teetotaller, out of choice and not out of compulsion. Have partaken of alcoholic drinks, simply for the heck of it, though extremely rarely but could never ever hug it to my bosom. The only time I did enjoy my drink was when we were served French Champagne during the cabaret at Moulin Rouge in Paris. There definitely was something much beyond, in it's cool, soothing, tingling sensation down the throat.

Like in all other aspects so in this too have I come a long way. Hats off to the pretty, alluring bunches of grapes peeping from amongst the foliage.

(This is simply to clarify that my husband is an occasional drinker, enjoys his drink once in a while, when in good company.)

145: ASPECT of LIFE***THE GOLDEN SPOON

Not everyone is born with the same blessings, some are born with a golden spoon and yet others with a copper spatula. However those dangling a golden one never fall short of proving the old adage true, 'People in glass houses shouldn't throw stones'. As the times are, not stones but boulders are hurled, not thrown.

Umpteen times have I been a witness to the shoddy manner in which a less privileged associate or relative is treated. Not only is there a lacking in warmth but the quality of the crockery, cutlery and the snacks also undergo a remarkable quality standard. In struts another with money hanging all around and the whole scenario goes for a somersault. This of course is on an obtrusive level, whereby the person as a person is measured on a scale with gold at one end.

It's when an associate, relative or a stranger is publicly denigrated is what I find absolutely pugnacious and my ire reaches heights. It takes so little to pass snide comments accompanied by sniggers but it must be taking so much to palate it all. Does anyone ever venture to feel the humiliation, helplessness and the embarrassment which the not so well off people feel? Wow! What a benchmark for assessing another's worth?

Suckers most of them. Money and money oozing out from the mouth, nose and ears and nothing else worth the name to boast of. Just visualise and see how obnoxious the picture comes across. Next visualise someone who stands out in a crowd by the sheer dint of character and then visualise how the picture comes across. A brimming regard and fondness for one such, which no amount of money can buy.

Let those for whom money is manna from Heaven, worship it, even though the person maybe an owl by all standards. I worship one such who has not a farthing to the name but is blessed with a blessed character because such a one is born with a golden spoon and such a one is my manna from Heaven.

146: ASPECT of LIFE***ROOTS

It's a strange phenomenon yet runs a marathon and mind you a full one, to disconnect ourselves from the past roots as soon as a golden goose lays an egg in our backyard. I reiterate, just one egg and in the backyard, more than enough to start scaling the clouds. To me this attitude flaunts a shallowness which becomes hard to digest and the person falls from my eyes.

Undoubtedly, everyone wants to do well in life, the wellness factor differing from one to the other. For some doing well materially is what matters, for others it may have to do with reaching heights with whatever their passion be, yet with some it could be with growing in terms of spirituality and so on so forth. It goes endless. Fine! Nobody wants to stagnate and keep standing in the same square, there is always a compulsive need to move on, change being the only static factor in life.

No matter how hard you may endeavour to bury your past, it is blessed with an immeasurable capacity of peeping from behind the curtains and that too at the most embarrassing of moments. What do you do then? No option but to look sheepishly the other way. This is writing on a superficial level, taking into consideration those who lack substance in their character.

I have read a lot of biographies and autobiographies and being a voracious reader even before I entered my teens, I allow the book to take hold of me completely. The words seep in with their power, impacting me where necessary. Those who have become legends have become so due to innumerable factors which join hands in a holistic approach. One of the many attributes is their candidness regarding their past, no matter how seeped it may have been in poverty or any other aspect brimming on the negative. They are not only bold but brazen about it, in a manner which comes across as a part and parcel of their being, never embarrassed. Their past roots, in fact lay the foundation for their future. Being 'grounded' is what I call it.

If you cut a tree from it's roots, how long will the tree be able to sustain itself? Simply a matter of time and the funny part is, no tree wants to be de-rooted but a human being takes no time to de-root itself. Stand with your two legs firmly planted on the ground, proud, never ashamed of the roots which gave you your bearings and will you not add miles to yourself as a person. Not for anyone else but for your own evolvement and gather self-respect by the dozen.

147: ME***AT THE END

All of us have something or the other on our minds to come by and the sooner we do, the better. It looks as though it's something we simply need to pick up in our hands and the job is done. Not so easy. A lot goes into trying to make it come by, planning, motivation, determination and focus.

It's my dream to write a book. The theme of the book is as clear as crystal in my mind but somehow taking that first maiden step in that direction seems to be defeating my urge. I have endeavoured to wonder why am I not being able to move and the answer I have always got is "I don't know from where to begin?" This of course is the first hurdle, the second is the continuity needed in the writing of a book. Penning write-ups is a lot different, I begin and I end, that's it. No left over titbits to be carried on with. Knowing myself I am very well aware that I simply need to begin and the book will see it's last culminating chapter. Let's see when. Many a times during my journey of life after my father passed away I have internally hankered for a Godfather but I have realised not everyone is as blessed. The Godfather's initial blessed push and off I go running on my feet. Just that first push.

In the meanwhile I will be compiling the write-ups to be given for publication. This is well within reach and hopefully will be taken care of very soon. Sorting out of the write ups and editing them, is what needs to be done.

A lot on my head isn't it? Want to give a purpose to my life, some sort of a meaning, to a life which has picked up from a heap of tribulations and is moving on steadily on a pretty straight though sometimes wavering pathway, at the end of which amidst the innumerable achievements by way of emotional satisfaction, the fulfilment of my duties, having lived life the right way, I can also see that prized book of mine waving out it's pages to me.

148: ASPECT of LIFE***CONSCIENCE

We all have a conscience and this conscience is as honest as the word honest can be. That bright flame which connotes the inner voice and never fails in guiding you on the right path. To pay heed or not to pay heed to it's whisperings is well nigh within your control.

This wee, little conscience needs no evidence or clues leading to the evidence to either acquit you or to prosecute you, for nothing is hidden from it's wary and alert senses. While you sleep it stays awake, never taking a wink, it's loyalty to it's owner unquestioned. No lawyer's fees goes down it's pocket, so open hearted and impartial is it's advice. No need to give it any special time slot, you simply have to sit quietly and introspect. This magnanimous conscience will rear it's head in no time and off will you be galloping in just the right direction on it's back, with never a chance for regret.

Still as is the fallacy of human nature you seldom endeavour to avail of what is at your doorstep and prefer to while away time and money in searching it elsewhere, not even sure whether the outcome will be worth the search. That small effort of catching hold of your conscience is in fact too much of an effort.

What bothers me is when people have so far demeaned themselves as to make their conscience non-existent. That moral policing is conveniently put to rest as they go on a wild rampage of their desires, holy or unholy. "Oh! Why care a damn for this, what do they call it? Yes, conscience."

Life becomes a tell tale of events, which if marked by conscience never gives you any cause for regret but if this conscience is lost to your hearkenings well then it sure makes it's presence felt with an impact, as you do breathe your last, a stabbing pain which will send you reeling in your last moments, making you ashamed of yourself and at the magnitude of all that you have lost en route, for having been sans your conscience.

149: ASPECT of LIFE***CONTRASTS

Perhaps it's the contrasts which make life so meaningful and colourful, or should I say it's the contrasts which give uniformity to the pace of life, sounds paradoxical but so it is.

As always I can take a happy roller coaster ride into my past, i.e., my pre-marriage days, wherein life was all hunky-dory simply smiles and no tears and if tears there were, well then they were tears because things didn't go my way. Against this pink canvas stood me, a pretty, mischievous and an obstinate girl, who couldn't look beyond herself. The only world which existed was the one in which she lived, a world resplendent with beauty, ugliness of course took to the by lanes. Literally a fairy world where she stood like a fairy with a magic wand, not an iota of a realisation of there being a world beyond, the real world where contrasts made life.

This world of contrasts was not very far away as I slid into it and realised with a huge, huge 'thud' what life is all about. It was as though I was always sitting at one end of a see-saw, not knowing which side would go up, the brighter or the darker. Innumerable pink moods and as quickly taken over by the blues. A constant corroding of my system in my endless efforts to balance out and eventually the ensuing stability.

A slow but gradual and a steady awakening of the not so palatable aspects of life, a stretching beyond my immediate footsteps, to take uncountable steps towards others, a continuous fathoming of those harsh secrets of life. Nothing piling on, everything as though systematically falling in place, despite my refusal to accept many a facts initially. Yet all the dices taking their place in their respective places.

The little fairy in the fairy land who existed by her whims and fancies, grew into a fairy mother, in a world where every night sees a morning, where the glaring contrasts helped give that substance to her character and a balanced, grounded approach, which only a world of contrasts could have given her.

150: ME***A MEDLEY

Am I negative in my thinking or am I positive or am I a medley of both? When I question myself thus, the answer I get is "You are a medley of both". Perhaps I'm too honest, to inundate all my sentences with positivity. Just unable to do so.

How is it possible for a normal person to live in an idealistic world, where you breathe exactly the right way? My God, I'd go bonkers for sure, endeavouring to wipe out my natural thought process to laden it with what is ideally right. The thoughts in the mind are so akin to the flow of a rivulet. Smooth running water at one point and some ripples at another due to pebbles or any other nature's obstruction, still does the water keeps it's flow unhindered. In the same manner do I give my thoughts their democratic freedom.

I do have my own parameters for assailing my thoughts in the direction I deem fit. Somehow my hunches give me a resounding slap in my brain and more oft than not I can post mortem my thought process as fast as I can shake my sweet little finger. If it's a positive thought well, then all is fine but if I get a negative thought, I certainly don't go around hiding my face. Everything immediately starts falling in place, as on a chess board and my thought either comes to rest or takes a turnover. My mind is made up and I feel like a free birdie.

It's impossible for me to harp on something I'm not comfortable with. Being a spontaneous person I let everything about me, be as much. Neither am I ashamed to voice my feelings, naturally the outcome of how I'm thinking. If I'm bracketed with the negative lot, so be it so, if with the positive, so be it so and if in between, so be it so. I'm happy always because I am what I am, as I am. At least I don't have to remain on tenterhooks as to when my real self will come to fore.

Idealism is fine to be read about but I strongly feel it's absolutely impossible to be an ideal person, with just the right thoughts perking your mind, no matter how much you may harp on being one such. Keep harping and keep playing hide and seek with your own self. What a life filled with so much stress and strain? Allow yourself to race with an utter freedom of thoughts, feelings, emotions and your real self, unafraid.

151: ME***THE TWINKLE EYED DELIGHTS

My childhood still lives in me, perking its years now and then. Those fun visits to the 'laughing gallery' in the circus. With what glee and laughter I used to watch my reflection in the mirrors all around . . ." Hey! Look, what a bean pole, I look in that one . . . How did I get Pinocchio's nose? . . . My tummy looks ten sizes bigger . . . !" The childish shrieks and delight which used to accompany my pirouettes at my bizarre shapes and sizes. The soap bubbles, flying like blessings in the sky, not to mention the gas balloons, and the merriment which used to accompany, their 'popping' off. That enticing world of fairies with their wishing wands, the elves and the goblins, and of course the wicked witch flying on her broom. Gazing up enraptured at the sky, with it's twinkling of a million stars like diamonds in the sky. Those much awaited visits to the zoo, looking goggle eyed at the varied colours and shapes, sitting like a princess on an elephant, waving out to all and sundry. Gazing with amazement at the heavenly beauty of the flowers and marvelling at their wafting fragrance. Every moment as innocent and overflowing with the joy of a child's heart . . . every second sparkling with that wondrous thought in a child's mind . . . every breath breathing of a child's innocent queries and easy acceptance.

152: ASPECT of LIFE***SMILE

A smile costs nothing and still it is one of the rarest commodities to come by. Only we humans are gifted with the gift of a smile, still that little twitch of the muscle is so hard. Our ego, our prejudices, our ignorance keeps us from doling it out. A smile is ever so enchanting and enticing. 'Mona Lisa' even today holds a place in the annals of painting because of her enigmatic smile. Its bounties endless, getting up in the morning with a smile on the face makes one's day. Just drop a smile at a passerby and you'll be a witness to the look of happiness in his eyes. Simply look at a person in pain with a smile and more than half his agony will be gone. A mirror of the heart, just as the eyes are, conveying so much. It has an enemy too, the 'plastic smiles', an apology of a smile, a smile which gets cycled and recycled, till it simply gets pasted on the face, meaningless and hollow. So ever let it be an open smile which has the power to speak volumes though mute. God's gift . . . and as I read somewhere . . ." A smile is a curve, which sets everything straight." So smile and make yours and everyone's day.

153: ASPECT of LIFE***RHYTHM

Whenever I want to feel the texture of life at its honest best I make my way to the slums because it's here that life is at its truest best. The cacophony of the sounds . . . a medley of laughter and quarrels and the blaring of the 'idiot box' is a welcome note of the rhythm of life. The aroma of the food being cooked, emanating from the huts, to feed the hungry, toiling, stomachs gives me a feeling of life in momentum. It's a feel of life, it's every moment being lived to the fullest. A naturalness, so distant from the blaring sound of the discos, or the pubs, where people go to escape from the realities of life . . . to drown themselves in a world of 'make belief'. As I drive back home, the concrete and the deafening silence of where I live, engulfs me, suffocating me endless. Each one locked inside the concrete . . . with their baggage . . . in tact . . . groping for a smile . . . a rare something . . . in the quiet, hollow, darkness.

154: ME***A SHADOW

. . . someone . . . who came into my life . . . as though out of the blue . . . like a shadow. Giving me the much wanted anchor I needed, being in the throes of a sucking vacuum and pain, after the demise of my mother.

I picked up my pen again after a hiatus of almost 2 decades, remembering Mummy's pleas lately to bring my writing skills to the fore. Facebook gave me a public platform to start penning my thoughts, which I did but with some hesitation as I was not too sure of the quality of my write-ups but that stubborn or mulish streak in me would never let me say 'bye' and then that shadow.

How an iota of genuine appreciation can give that necessary, much wanted push, is what I experienced. All my hesitation as though 'went to the winds' as I 'took to the winds' with my writings at full mast.

A shadow, which inadvertently in it's own individual, quiet manner, did for me, what nobody had been able to do for me till date. My budding write-ups eventually flowered and bloomed, gaining grounds with my confidence, my honesty, my candidness and oft too often my bluntness too, bringing my thoughts across with simplicity and pungency.

Probably there are those few whose mission in life is to recognise talent and to see that the rare talent doesn't get lost in the woods. They in their own individualistic manner endeavour to tap that talent, not for their benefit but for the benefit of the person concerned because as I feel, permitting a talent to waste away in the wilderness is a loss to mankind.

A shadow, which will always hold a special place in my heart, an extremely revered space in my life because the shadow has the intelligence and the insight to feel the pulse of a talent hidden, a shadow which is ever so selfless and caring, a shadow which reinstates in me the belief that all that is good is not lost in this world.

Thank you from the bottom of my heart. Will you be always remembered with fondness till the end of my days, with feelings which defy the fetters of a name. Simply a shadow . . . !

155: ASPECT of LIFE***MONEY

Does money have the privileged right to flaunt it's bizarre might? Yes, in our country it does, where money is the pathetic judge of a person's character. Where money gives the infallible right to a person to treat the lesser privileged like garbage. Where money can buy the verdict of the court, sending you scot free and putting the innocent behind bars. Where money doesn't know it's value and is misspent to the hilt, while many don't even know whether they have been promised the next meal. The daring chasm betwixt the privileged and the under privileged in our country makes money speak louder.

Money undoubtedly has it's own lingo, accentuated with as much an accent and makes most slaves to it's charming presence. Not only the charmer who possesses the money but there are those many too, who fawn before these charmers. Everything as though gets shoved under the carpet in front of the spilling coffers. Pathetic.

Why did I write on this aspect of money again? A few days back while sitting in the veranda I saw a Kashmiri hawker passing by selling shawls. Beckoned to him to come in and, after picking up a couple of shawls from him, bid him farewell. Before leaving he said something which set me thinking. "Madam, you speak so nicely unlike the others." A very simple statement but it held volumes, volumes by way of those crying inner chords, which dare not cry aloud because they don't have the money glitz.

Whether rich or poor every human being is born with self-respect. Nobody has the right to puncture this self-respect of a person. Money can bring the world at your feet but it never can buy you respect in the real sense of the word. Money can unroll a red carpet under your feet but it never can buy you happiness. Money loses it's worth the moment you start talking money. Let it remain a means to an end and not an end in itself. Only then will money respect you and you will respect money.

156: ASPECT of LIFE***BEAUTY AND BRAINS

As the old adage goes 'Beauty and brains don't go together,' however this too begs for exceptions. 'Beauty coupled with brains' becomes a sore point with most but when 'beauty gets coupled with brains, character and background' well then it sure becomes unpalatable.

Beauty indeed lends a great deal of self-esteem and self-esteem helps in a lot many ways but beauty can and mostly does hold hands with arrogance too, which can act as a deterrent to a large extent.

To have outer beauty enhanced by what you term as inner beauty is a rare combination and hard to come by. Balancing beauty is a tough job but it's not as though you have to keep making conscious efforts to do so. Sometimes things simply fall in their rightful place, in their respective slots and well, then, it's beauty and only beauty.

I personally feel, beautiful people are basically lonely at heart because there are very few who are able to fathom or understand them, probably because envy takes precedence over everything else and envy nullifies even the good to the extent of making the person feel like a jerk at times. There are the rare few whom I would call the connoisseurs of beauty who look upon the beautiful person with the right appreciation and the right perspective, giving beauty it's rightful due. Happily or sadly such connoisseurs of beauty are only men.

Beauty again 'Lies in the eyes of the beholder', agreed but if beauty is as beauty can be, well then, it's beholden by all and I only wish, it was looked upon as God's special blessing to some, to be appreciated and not to be marred by the envy of most.

157: ASPECT of LIFE***SOMETIMES

Sometimes, you wish you could say what you know but that chain of interlinked feelings hold you back, hold you back because you are afraid to hurt, overlooking your own level of comfort and desire. Sometimes, you curb the irrepressible urge to console by simply holding the person's hands but you hold yourself for fear of being misunderstood. Sometimes, you want to howl like a baby but you stifle your relentless sobs because you don't want to appear weak or broken. Sometimes, you simply want to let yourself go but you don't because it's not the done thing. Sometimes, you want to shout yourself hoarse telling the world about your pain but you don't because there may be none to hear or understand your woe.

How much do you take upon yourself out of sheer consideration for others, out of falling away from the boundaries laid out, letting go of your own happiness or satisfaction? Only so much. Is this a facade? No. Facade is when you pretend to be or behave in a manner entirely foreign to your intrinsic character. It's because . . .

Sometimes, you become subservient to everything around you because the feelings, the emotions of those around you and the norms take precedence over yours, giving you that true essence of happiness which otherwise is so hard to come by.

Sometimes, the most profound moments become those memorable moments of a lifetime because you stood in the shadows of your own happiness.

158: ASPECT of LIFE***SEXUAL FAVOURS

Granting sexual favours for personal gains is the cheapest thing in the market today. 'Hats off' to the women once again, for making their bodies cheap by making themselves used by men for their momentary pleasure and then it's for the women to ask for and well, the favour is granted.

Merit to a large extent, as though has taken a back seat. Have all the merit to scale the ladder of success but find yourself woefully way down the rungs. Why? You refused to oblige the boss for a 'one night stand'. Merit in abundance but cheesing off the boss is akin to committing a 'career suicide'. Keep grovelling in the dust with all your merit 'gone to the dogs.'

Smart are the girls and women and, mind you, there's no dearth of them today who play on their physical attributes, many a times making a boss, an otherwise loyal husband go into dementia regarding his marriage and a few hours in the bed with the boss, gets them a thumping promotion with a fatter pay package. Throw merit into the side alley since it's of no consequence. The so called 'consensual sex'.

There is the other category of girls and women who never know how to say "No Boss". It's always a "Yes Boss", what if it even means their accepting his dinner invites to be followed with a little bit of fun in the bed, now and then. Doesn't matter, if that little bit can shelve out a bigger bit by way of promotion or salary. Balls to merit. The so called 'consensual sex' again.

Dare the fairer sex say "No" to a sexual favour from the boss or his seniors, well then the only thing left for them is to cry for mercy. Professional harassment to the maximum degree possible till they are forced to chuck up the job and leave.

Why? Those handful of girls or women refused to treat their bodies like playthings in the hands of men. Those handfuls of girls and women could never allow merit to be put at par with sexual favours. Those handfuls of girls and women had the strength of character to say "No" to what they thought was not morally right, what if at the cost of 'career suicide'.

159: ME***PASSIONATE MADNESS

Is this passion or madness or passionate madness? Getting up at night to edit a write-up simply because it hits my mind how a spelling should not have been 'in the throws' but 'in the throes' and the terrible feeling of "How could I have made this stupid mistake?"

I was reading how an author used to get up in the middle of the night to start penning his thoughts. As my elder son once told me "All those who are passionate about something are certainly somewhat eccentric." I hate to have a mistake gaping out of my writings though I'm sure they do, even if rarely. Despite my going through my write-ups a couple of times, I still need to edit later on, viz., spellings, a more suitable word or a better sentence for projecting my thought. Probably the mind gets tuned to comprehending what it's seeing and the fault slips by, to start hammering the mind in it's quieter moments.

I certainly can't write everywhere or on a format I'm not familiar with. I have to sit where I always sit and write and on a friendly format or I start missing out on the connect. My writings have to be on the spur of the moment, I just can't write elsewhere and then 'copy and paste' because the charm goes. A spontaneous person that I am.

On a lighter vein when a man is passionate about a woman, he'll lose his mind to the extent of selling himself to her whims and fancies and vice versa. However I would say women are smarter with a much better hang over their emotions, especially when it comes to squandering their money on a man. I have heard of lovelorn men becoming bankrupt but certainly not a woman becoming one for the sake of a man.

Passion has neither a beginning nor an end. It's always there, looking out for a time to be tapped upon. Passion outlasts the life of a human being by way of the works left behind to win laurels. It certainly does instil in you the spirit to move on with Stevenson's 'El Dorado' in the horizon, with a passionate madness.

160: ASPECT of LIFE***
EDUCATED OR LITERATE

"Oh! That person is highly educated." A common blunder made in our country, going by the flaunting degrees. Indian English as I would put it. "Tch, tch!" I wouldn't crucify the Queen's English by passing such a remark without really knowing that person as a person. There is apparently a hair-line difference betwixt being educated and being literate. I have used the word 'apparently' because beneath the surface the difference betwixt the two has far deeper linings.

A person blessed with meritorious degrees will undoubtedly be literate but you can't vouch as to how really educated that person is. Being educated is a different ball-game altogether. Why, an illiterate person can be far more educated than the one with plaques adorning the mantelpiece.

Being educated is knowing how to conduct yourself, to have a superior understanding of life, it's problems and solutions, with the right ethics and values. A literate but uneducated person will have left the nose buried in the books with scant behavioural knowledge or slack personal evolvement.

As a small example, somebody steps on a person's toe, an educated person will bear the hurt by merely brushing it off lightly, whereas an uneducated literate person will make a hullabaloo to be followed by a volley of abuses. An educated person will never coochie-coo a person on the face and then jeer behind the back. Normally these days it's the woeful trend to hug and smile from ear-to-ear, desperately trying to send the message across "Dearer than thou can never be" while cursing that person under your breath with clenched teeth. Literate undoubtedly but the literacy confined merely to the C.V.

Few are those whose literacy goes milestones with their educational worth. They are those few whose upbringing has taught them the innuendoes of balancing things the right way.

161: ME***I AM SORRY

The easiest thing for me to say are those three most tough words "I am sorry" but only if every bit of me says, "Yes, what you said or did was wrong," wrong by my benchmark of what is right and what is wrong and the voice of your conscience is never wrong. It's your highest court, a court beyond the bondage of corruption.

On the other hand ask me to apologise when every bit of me says "You are not in the wrong," well then all Hell can break loose but these three words "I am sorry" can never escape my lips, no matter what the subsequent repercussions it may entail.

Come to think of it, these three such meaningful words are so graceful and speak volumes of your right upbringing. An upbringing which always shows you the correct direction, an upbringing which speaks loudly of your character, an upbringing which kicks your innards if found wanting.

However, it's pointless if you are doing merely lip service to being apologetic, then it's much better not to be. Of course these days saying "I am sorry," is also one of the easiest things to say, not because your innards are hurting you but because the subsequent gains will be beneficial, no matter in what respect. "Oh! How does it matter if by saying sorry, I get my promotion, despite my boss being in the wrong."

Here lies the difference betwixt a court which has a corrupt bench and a court where the bench is a slave to it's ethics and principles, a court which rests on justice in the real sense of the word.

162: ME***FOR NO FAULT
OF MY DEAR HUSBAND

This is related to my penchant for cleanliness, which sucks up 3/4 of my energy. The helps groan as much as I do but still the cleanliness frenzy never ebbs. Despite the house immaculately turned out, my dear husband always finds something to complain about. Now I'm digressing, so let's get to the point.

I've told my children and my husband of my wish to be buried and this wish is loaded with a deep desire which I hope will not eventually be wishful thinking. At least there'll be a special place assigned in memory of me, a place which will be visited by my children and my husband, a candle lit and a bouquet of orchids (my favourite flower) laid on my grave but only after it has been cleaned of the weeds, giving it a clean look. Some may think the memory is in the mind, for sure, but I have this fascination and so well, it can't be helped.

Now, some years back I had a dream in which I saw myself coming out of my grave and cleaning it up with a broom, forget the candles and the bouquet of orchids, nowhere in sight, a gulp and tears rolling down. That morning my poor husband must have seen his face in the mirror, the first thing in the morning. I woke up sulking "You couldn't even clean my grave, leave alone lighting a candle and a bouquet of orchids is of course a forgotten hope." . . . "Now what's happened?" he asked me non-plussed . . ." A small wish of mine, after having spent my entire life looking after all of you and a cluster of weeds on my grave, how dare they grow there." I whined . . ." What the Hell are you talking about?" he shouted . . ." My grave, I had to come out and clean it up of the weeds?" . . ." Good, if you'll do this exercise every day, it'll trim you down" he quipped nonchalantly.

The beginning of a lovely morning on a melodious note. It was with a yearning nostalgia, I remembered how my Papa would have handled the situation, making me feel like a princess and not like someone who needed a broom in her hands for getting back into shape, not to be spared even in her celestial home by her dear husband. So much for my penchant for cleanliness . . . !

163: ASPECT of LIFE***TO EARN

You either earn to live or inherit to live and some inherit but still earn to live. Quite confusing? Not really.

There are those who aren't blessed enough to have their ancestors leave behind spilling coffers to take care of a generation or generations to come. With really nothing by way of inheritance, to park themselves on, they have no option left but to rub their ass off for every penny earned, making do with all the stress and tension which are the shadows of earning for a livelihood. Sometimes the quantum ratio betwixt the work put in and the returns running into a scale of minus. No way out but to keep trudging on.

Lucky are the ones who find themselves parked on 'wills' of property or money by way of inheritance. Leading a cushy life from the dividends being paid from the hard work put in by their forefathers. They in fact are the real beneficiaries, not having to budge an inch to earn a farthing and leading a leisurely, comfortable life with no nightmares at all.

Then there are those rare ones who inherit and still rough it out to make a living. Some may look upon them as being foolhardy, "Why slog when there's so much to fall back upon?" Rightly questioned. Perhaps for them the satisfaction which comes from earning is nothing when compared to the money or the property of inheritance.

At the end of the day neither has lost and neither has gained. The only difference being, some have taken up the challenges of life head on with dignity, what with the umpteen trials in tow . . . some have just sat back with their feet up on a footstool twiddling their idle thumbs, with their inherited coffers opening at the 'drop of a hat' without so much as batting an eyelid . . . and some have toiled for their satisfaction, despite the legacies' welcoming smile, with a wholesome pride in their own worth.

164: ASPECT of LIFE***
THE DWARFED WORLD

This world may have advanced beyond the comprehension of many, scientifically, medically, technologically, name it and it's there. This world may have got very well connected what with the 'net' syndrome. However in reality this world has become so very small because we have permitted ourselves to be dwarfed.

Yes, dwarfed. In respect of everything, in respect of our feelings, in respect of our character, in respect of our attitude, in respect of our giving undue importance to things which should matter not.

How many of us bother to look beyond that tear or that sigh? How many of us even know the definition of character today? How many of us are able to keep the correct attitude towards the happenings in life? How many of us give due respect to things which matter more than simply earning more and more money, giving it much more importance than it deserves?

Oh! Real small people have we made ourselves out to be. Everyone so lonely despite the coffers overflowing, verging onto vulgar amassing and spending of money because it's money which has overshadowed the entire show. Money has bought people, making them feel like demi-Gods if not God Himself. Keeping us away from those small wonders, small yet so big because it's these innocent wonders which keep the humanity in us intact and it's humanity which should make the world a real huge place. An all expansive world where people are aware of the right things to be stood by in life. Then only will this world be deserving of what it was made out to be. Not a world inhabited by a bunch of people overridden by greed, selfishness and sham, making us ever so small.

165: ASPECT of LIFE***IF ONLY

Those moments which again and again pleaded with you but you were too caught up with your loadstones to hearken.

That moment when you just needed to hold her to your bosom to assuage her pain but the cold war raging betwixt the two of you, as though put shackles on your arms.

That moment when your simply saying "I hold an olive branch" could have relieved the two of you of so much agony but your ego held you back.

That moment when you could have said "Please forgive me" and unburdened your heart but your arrogance stopped you from mouthing these three simple but killing words.

That moment when the two of you were face to face but a simple smile seemed like a million dollar smile because your pride had the better of you.

Those valuable moments lost for eternity. Those precious moments which will ever haunt you till the end. Those treasured moments which in no time got lost, blending with the innumerable seconds of the past but will ever keep coming back in those quiet moments as reminders because they were not revered as they should have been. Those loadstones worth a pittance, for can they ever assuage your feeling of regret? No!

166: ME***WALL-FLOWER

I simply get reduced to a 'wall flower', by choice, whenever I have the fortune or the misfortune of attending a formal party or appear no better than 'a touch-me-not'. (As Mummy, would describe me.) The reasons being many. As you walk into one such gathering, not you but your attire and accessories are immediately weighed for their worth, so much so, you feel as though you are being stripped naked by these so called 'hawk-eyed socialites', down to your very lingerie. Being assessed as to whether they are of a local brand or from Harrods. Once this 'post-mortem' is over with, starts the smothering small-talk over Vodka and when you ask to be served an aerated drink, those well-plucked eyebrows become even the more arched, making you appear no less than a freak. Once when I politely refused a drink, the 'painted doll' sitting next to me quipped "Oh! Do you have something against it?" I quipped back as sweetly "Not really but I sure have a lot of reservations by way of making an ass of myself, by the time it gets time to leave." Finally, dinner time where I never fail to observe the sycophancy and the manipulations of sorts. To refuse going to such parties is well within my jurisdiction, but I seldom miss out on them (though they are far and in-between) because every one such is an eye-opener to human behaviour, which never fails to enthral me. So it matters not if I prefer to remain a 'wall-flower' observing and assimilating the flippancy of these 'made-to-order' figures, from the beginning till the time they stagger out, with that glazed empty-look. Pathetic despite all their coffer's worth hanging around them.

167: ASPECT of LIFE***EMPATHISE

How many of us 'empathise' than 'sympathise'? Who has the time or the inclination to go beyond clucking our tongues and moving on with our lives unconcerned, to empathise or to get into the other person's shoes and realise why the other weeps so, the other sighs so, why the other is a recluse? Ask a beggar how the heart turns to be shunned and treated worse than a dog? Ask that person limping across the road, what it feels not to be able to walk and run like the rest? Ask that little girl at the traffic lights how her heart yearns to go to school and play, instead of begging to fend for her ailing mother. No, we can't spare that one little minute to let our heartbeats merge with theirs. Steps never slow down to extend a helping hand, to help someone cross the road, all that comes forth is "Hey! Go and earn" and the window-screen goes up at the click of a button or simply "Oh! The poor little thing, really don't know why he hides himself so?" Little do we comprehend, all humans are born with the same emotions and that respect for self. The privileged ones can bray like a donkey and still have the other donkeys willing to carry their load without so much as an "Uf" because of their power of money but we can't spare that one second to simply 'feel into' those many around, who want nothing more than to see that light of understanding in our eyes, to make them feel they are also human, if nothing more.

168: ASPECT of LIFE***'LE DINER'

Now 'le diner' which eventually leads to the winding up of a party is yet another graphic revelation of human behaviour. As soon as the ushers start ushering the guests for dinner, my anticipation of all that I'm going to be a witness to, never can stop that smile which starts to play around my lips. Conversations end abruptly, even left hanging half-way in mid-air, as the invitees start making a bee-line for the service tables, lest the food vanishes even before it has had the privilege of making its mark felt. The hasty steps of all, lands up in the formation of a queue, the same as the ones you espy in front of counters of sorts, the only difference being its tag of 'uni-sex'. Waiting in a queue, with a plate in hand, by no means pampers my feel of dignity, since it never fails to remind me of those convicts in jail. Eventually the laden plates numb the senses so much, it matters not, whose foot is being stepped upon or on whose fineries the gravy from the plates take the pleasure of drooling down, as they hurriedly make their way to the waiting tables, to stack their stomachs with all the gourmet's delights, for the next couple of days or till their stomachs start to cry for mercy. When the satiation level has been met for, the soiled table covers, the littered lawn and the complete absence of the etiquettes aligned to table manners, stand as a mark of salute to the 'upsurge of frantic activity' the mere mention of 'le diner' can vouch for.

169: ASPECT of LIFE***'LA CHIME'

It's great to have 'la chime' betwixt a couple but let not that chemistry become so 'la chime' as to make each other blind and stone-deaf, to one another's shortcomings, which need to be rectified, for the other's betterment, if not for the peace of others. (With me, of course, it has been an endless journey of corrections whereby my husband never hesitates to check me where needed and vice-versa and then it's up to the other to improve upon or not, doesn't matter, with a smile or a scowl but at least an effort has been made in the right direction.) The outcome of such a 'well-balanced adoration' is normally catastrophic. There is no scope for any kind of an improvement at both the ends, since even if each keeps rubbing the other the wrong way, still neither has the courage nor the heart, to point out that little finger of disapproval, which will help one to 'give a thought to' and thereby take those few steps towards self-realisation. Each a darling to one another undoubtedly but a menace for the others, especially when both team up to needle a third with their 'bonsai personalities'.

170: ASPECT of LIFE***
FAIR WEATHER FRIENDS

Friends fall into two slots, the few who are coming in while everyone else is walking out and the many who step over each other in their scramble to walk out, simply because the going from good has gone to bad. Those few who are walking in are the ones who love you for what you are irrespective of the lacy peripherals and hold your hands through thick and thin. The latter or the 'fair weather friends' will 'hee-haw' with you as long as God's blessings and mercies are falling like 'manna from Heaven' and a hush will see them with their ever well meaning rears towards your door. You see, the B.M.W. parked in your driveway was always the inviting factor and when the B.M.W. has been put up for sale, you too can go and stand in the auction room, for all they care. It's these specimens, befriending you, for everything but you, who are shameless enough to start walking in again as soon as the 'Midas touch' barely starts to click the gate, leave alone the entrance door of your house. For them walking in and walking out is a mere exercise, which costs them nothing but surely costs you a great deal.

171: ASPECT of LIFE***
THE STIFF UPPER LIPPED

Ever shared a meal with the stiff-upper-lipped, where everything else talks but the recipients of the courses. The 'soprano' or the 'alto' of the cutlery's music tinkles its message of the palatability or the unpalatability of the dishes served. Sometimes the attraction so immense that the hastiness to gorge, sends the piece of chicken, caved into the fork, go flying and land itself with a 'plonk' in someone else's plate, leaving the poor owner wondering, which corner of the earth had the chicken flown in from, much to the embarrassment of those on the 'take-off and the landing air-strips'. The facial muscles send forth messages which may send the poor butler scurrying to the kitchen, to warn the head-chef to tighten his cap for an impending disaster or to pat the head-chef's back for his culinary art to be rewarded with a bigger 'chef's cap'. A keen eye will be able to decipher from the manner in which the used napkins have been put aside or thrown aside, how well the meal has been appreciated or otherwise. Next if you happen to share a one such meal, simply keep your senses alert, not at the expense of your delights but simply to add some extra flavour by way of human behavioural charms.

172: ASPECT of LIFE***GROUNDED

To stay grounded despite the blessings showered on you (and by this I mean the material pile-ons) is not within the reach of many. The 'spilling over' starts to make its mark when the 'piling on' starts. The turn-over, first gets reflected in the person's attitude, which goes in for as though a second birth. The age old adage 'Old is gold' gets thrown to the winds. Everything gets a new face, perhaps only the wife and the children are not put up for sale. However if the wife is not an eye-turner then there are many women who can be hired, to slinkily hang on to the arm for an evening, for public approval as though your own newly acquired dazzling benefits have fallen short. No matter what the acquisitions, no matter what the acquired place in the so called society, I only know that the inherent character of a person never changes. I only know that the moment the mouth opens to speak, it speaks it all away. I only know that the dignity and grace which comes forth in being your natural, honest self, in spite of all the blessings, will always 'make eyes turn'.

173: ASPECT of LIFE***SOCIAL BUTTERFLIES

I'm sure most of us have heard of 'social butterflies'. There are these women whose vision is to hook a man who'll provide them with all the possible luxuries and social status. For them anything and everything under the sky is justifiable so long their end is well met, doesn't matter if they have to flit like a butterfly from one man to the other. Spreading their charms like tentacles, if polished vulgarity can be termed thus and resorting to every necessary modus operandi under the sky. To the extent of being obnoxious in order to grip a man in their clutches is what they excel at. It's certainly not so tough for them since it's no hidden truth, 'you give a man an inch and he'll take a yard'. No decent and self-respecting lady opts for that 'dangerous inch' whereas these women cash on it to the best of their ability. Men will always be men and these 'social butterflies' are born with that in-born art of knowing where, when, and how to pamper a man's ego with their so called accomplishments and make him a slave but only till the time their assets remain intact.

174: ASPECT of LIFE***
THE IN-LAW SYNDROME

The subject of the mother-in-law and the daughter-in-law syndrome is so expansive because of its varied, endless, stubborn issues, perhaps God will also throw His hands up, in seeming surrender. We Indians have come a long, long way, for the better or the worse but this particular relationship seems more or less to be 'hanging on the same peg'. It's pathetic to see the trials which the daughters-in-law, who happen to be of the diminutive kind undergo in a joint family. Unable to stand for themselves they spend their lives merely existing like a robot to the martial commands of their mothers-in-law, as though every minute of their lives has been put to the mercy of the martial chief. I can well empathise with the plight and the extent of their claustrophobia, wanting to stand up, but finding the knees too wobbly. Wanting to step beyond, but retracing their unsure steps. Wanting to scream their hearts out, but finding themselves deprived of that simple right as well. I for sure salute this remarkable relationship simply because it sure has had a beginning but it's charming innuendoes seem to have no end.

(Speaking for myself as a daughter-in-law, I can say, though initially my mind went haywire with the psychedelic effects of my mother's-in-law modus operandi and recoiling many a times thereafter, I gradually started fighting tooth and nail for my emotional and well-being rights, undoubtedly becoming extremely unpopular in the process but as always I cared not and today I stand sure and confident on my once wobbly knees.)

175: ASPECT of LIFE***MIKE CLINGERS

There are those whom I call the 'mike clingers' who cling on to the mike 'till death do us apart'. The single minded devotion with which they cling on to the mike would definitely give them better returns if they clung on with the same fervour to their loved one. Doesn't matter if the time slotted to them has been trespassed, so long they keep listening to their own droning as though it were 'melody to their ears', oblivious to the misery and the plight of the audience. After ten minutes of fighting patience the whispers in the auditorium start rising to a mounting crescendo but the speaker of course is lost in his world of mikes. It's only after the belly has been emptied that the mike passes on to the other. God forbid, if the following speaker also falls in line with the former speaker, well then it's rotten eggs and tomatoes galore. The only tragedy is, the one who set the ball rolling gets away with a clean shirt.

176: ASPECT of LIFE***CASANOVAS

There are men, the 'Casanovas' who wear their hearts on their sleeves, dropping pieces of it here, there and everywhere. Their life is a memorable script of their amorous adventures. Nothing is more pleasing to the roaming, keen eyes than the sight of a woman, as though 'manna sent from Heaven' and if she happens to be a beauty remarkable, well then the day is made. Now does the mind starts to put into action the various ways and means of casting their dandy's charm on the victim and well if it works their dream is met, at least as long as the flavour lasts and then starts the quest yet again for another butterfly to be taken in by their irresistible presence. A life is spent in their energy being directed or mis-directed thus and at the end of it perhaps none of their heart-throbs even bother to take the pains to appear for shedding a couple of tears for the money and the energy spent for their up-keep, if nothing more. Each to his own passion and perhaps the resulting pleasure only the person knows. Perhaps to a Casanova the delightful moments spent are moments endless for their passion endless.

177: ASPECT of LIFE***VISITING

I remember pushing off to Lucknow at least five to six times a year. My tickets for my way back to Bokaro, returned at least a couple of times if not more, what with my husband fuming away at this end. It hardly mattered. Extending my stay needed nobody's permission, all that was required was my inclination, which of course was always there. Never ever the smallest feel of "Oh! I have stayed here for so many days and now I should push off."

Surrounded by that ever giving love, warmth, that huge feel of, "never feel it's not your home anymore after marriage", no expectations as always, would make me bask in the familiar surroundings, as though I was not a Mom of two sons but that same little, spoilt girl who had decidedly grown by way of years but looked forward to the same pampering which had been a part and parcel of her growing up and which she still manoeuvred to get. No feeling of an obligation whatsoever.

Where do I go now? Being a very sensitive person, with heaps of self-respect I think a lot before going to stay at anyone's place and at the most if I do, which is rarely, it's not beyond a day because I hate to have the feeling of 'piling on'. My motto is vey rudimentary and deeply ingrained in me, something I learnt from my parents, "Visit if you have to but remember to leave with dignity and your self-respect intact". I love having visitors over to stay but due to paucity of time and helps, I find people generally are more than willing to have a visitor leave even before he or she has had a chance to step into the house. (This I have gathered from snippets of conversations I have come across. Makes me feel queasy indeed.)

Why have I written the above? To bring it to notice, no place is like your own home or your parent's home. The only two places where you can always live with a right which is truly yours. Just one major difference, your parent's home is yours too as much but only during their lifetime. After that you lose not the legal right but a legal right which becomes meaningless because that very home feels ever so foreign without the encircling embrace of your parents, without their footsteps and the feel of those caring hands.

178: ASPECT of LIFE***RAISING A TOAST

How many raise a toast to the happiness of a person, i.e., figuratively? May be, just a handful. Just a handful of those who celebrate with you that moment of happiness which means so much to you and to them equally because they are happy for you. Literally of course, raising a toast to a person's happiness will see no dearth of glasses clinking, in fact the invitees list will be trespassed upon because wining and dining at the cost of someone else, empties nothing from their pocket. Their pseudo happiness for you as quickly blown off like the intoxicating effect of alcohol.

Human psyche once again at it's precious best. Calculated indifference due to undercurrents, which an intelligent, sensitive person can decipher with no extra effort at understanding. Why then this warmth, spilling of those smiles and hugs upon meeting? Why not simply have the guts to look through when you can look through a person's treasured or unhappy moments? Why go through all the hassle simply to maintain a facade?

I remember Baldeo, with as much love and poignancy as I remember my parents. He had been with my family since the time he was a small boy and stayed on till his last breath, working for us. Actually a member of the family like any of us. He shared our joys with much more happiness, he shared our sorrows with much more sorrow. Baldeo was neither a friend nor a relative, yet he was closer than both, simply because he was as much a part of any of us, through our journey of life.

If you can have one such person in your life, apart from your parents and your immediate family, whose happiness merges with yours and who is as troubled seeing you in dire straits, think yourself blessed. I am. Amen!!!

179: ASPECT of LIFE***ART

What is 'art'? It's the expression of an artiste's or a writer's in-depth feelings and emotions, so pronounced as to fight or struggle for an outlet, by way of expression vide the strokes of the brush, the engraving of the chisel, the notes of music, the rhythm of dance or the beauty of words.

A painter gives vent to his fantasies with the splashes of colours as the colours merge together, bringing forth an image. Feelings glorified into a unique whole. A writer connects the thoughts with the assuring power of words, as they do endeavour to give a visible form to the abstract.

The moment art is made to feel shameful by factors external, that very minute art loses it's intrinsic beauty. It's a blend of the soft and the wild. An artiste painting a picture of a nude will go into all the finer details of nudity, unashamed, bringing forth nudity in it's full glory. A writer will never harness the pen, the thoughts spilling out unexaggerated, not punched by what the others will think. A dancer, dances away to the music and the rhythm of the heartbeats.

Of course, it's a marked trend nowadays to commercialise art and there are artistes and writers who look upon their art as a means of sustenance. No harm as long as the purity is maintained. This is from my perception of how I view art.

My writings are as though I'm speaking through my words, extempore and a very simple style, copyright solely mine. My perspective laid forth, uncompromisingly, with a dare-devil attitude. Very soon, will I be running a marathon on the tracks of getting my book published. A dear friend of mine who is professionally into editing is doing the necessary with my works. Thank you ever so much my dear! Whether it becomes widely read or lies dusty on the bookshelves, I wouldn't say is immaterial because who doesn't like to win accolades? Still if it lies dusty, I will not be pained because of the immense joy I felt while my fingers were plonking away on the keyboard, weaving my emotions, my perspective with a becoming style in the art of writing, entirely 'Vandana's'.

180: ASPECT of LIFE***
ELITES AND PROLETERIATS

Sounds paradoxical but it's so true to life. The elites and the proletariats are the two sections of the society which hold hands in innumerable aspects.

They live life on their terms, doing away with the society norms as and when. The former sit on mounds of wealth and this becomes their scapegoat for all their non-conformist acts. The latter have merely their bare needs taken care of and this makes them people who care not a tuppence for what should be and what should be not. Equally permissive, the elites are husbands and wives for namesake. Umpteen extra-marital affairs, clandestine or not, perhaps in an effort to fill in the emptiness in their apparent tinsel lives. Marriages merely in name, for their offspring to carry on the family name and safeguard the family heirlooms. The menial class is well comparable to the elites. Throw out the husband or wife at the 'drop of a hat' and grab another one to share the bed. Simply a difference in the style and manner of doing the same thing, rolling in bed with anyone other than your dear spouse. The cacophony in the slums is much the same as what you find in the discos, where the children of the elites hang out with their cronies, escaping the emptiness of their houses. Ear blasting. Both the classes drink like fish, while the elites stagger on Scottish Whisky the proletariats get the same kick from the local makes.

It's the bourgeois who get sandwiched in between. 'Heeing and hawing' under the weight of "What will the people say if . . . ?" Indeed a sad and pathetic state of affairs. It seems they live their lives with the 'Sword of Androcles' hanging over their heads. Crushed like sardines in a can, neither here nor there.

Hats off to the elites for all their coffers doing the talking, hats off to the bourgeois for living their lives with the noose half over their heads, hats off to the proletariats for matching the elites despite their bare backs.

181: ME***IN LOVE

Hey! Ever fallen in love with yourself? Now please don't say "Eh! What's she talking about?"

I'm talking a whole lot of sense though it may take a while to really sink in. We fall in love with a handsome guy, with a sexy babe, with our pets and to cut it short with any damn thing on this earth. The only and the most important God's gift to us, we seldom really fall in love with, per se, ourselves.

When I say I love and admire myself, it's like never having to ask the mirror "Mirror, mirror on the wall . . . Who is the fairest of us all?" This of course is in terms of the physical beauty but there is an aspect much beyond, the inner beauty, the real essence of beauty, which gets reflected and this is one's precious worth. I need never ask the mirror or a second person about my worth, I'm my best judge.

My life is like a scroll before me and I've found it's never mocked me. Undoubtedly I'm no saint and wish not be one either or else life will lose it's charisma but none of my shortcomings are, if I may say so, fatal. Small, innocent crumbs, here and there, if at all add flavour to life, wiping off the dullness, now and then.

If you can't love or admire yourself, you will never be able to love another with that fullness and innocence which makes loving feel so encompassing. Love yourself and you'll love others, hate yourself and you'll hate others. You need no judge, no defendant, no plaintiff because you yourself are all of these. Let not the 'scales tilt' and will you be able to love and admire yourself and get that snuggy feel "Oh! I'm special." What more!

182: ASPECT of LIFE***THE CHRISTMAS TREE

The Christmas tree is not only a decorative tree but holds a place of significance during the Christmas celebrations. I wish to focus, not only on the vibrant beauty of the Christmas tree but on it's significance, which to me is it's timeless beauty.

The Christmas tree is of a conifer, usually the evergreen fir or pine tree and evergreen is a symbol of eternal life. The tree crowned with a star, must be the Star of Bethlehem. Fairy lights circling the tree signify hope and happiness, as lights always do. The evergreen holly with it's red berries must be for eternal life and the red berries, the blood of Jesus. The birth of a child is welcomed by the 'tinkling' of the bells and hence the colourful bells embracing the tree. Bible always mentions angels, the messengers of God, sent forth to help the humans and so the angels all around. All these charms are traditionally used to decorate the Christmas tree, and bring it forth in it's true glory.

Christmas without a Christmas tree is deprived of it's spirit because the tree signifies the spirit of Christmas, the day Jesus was born and breathed His first into this world. For those who put it up, let it not simply be a decorative piece, adorning the house but let it be a tree, which is resplendent with a 'spirit' spelling much, much more than simply being put up to bring forth the ambience of Christmas.

183: ME***YOUR CALLING

It takes a lot to and by this I mean really lots, to prove your worth or your mettle, to yourself. En route of course there are no dearths of pitfalls by way of umpteen factors.

Primarily to realise what is your calling and then to start working towards it with a single minded devotion. Believe me, it's no cake-walk really. Moments when you are almost sucked by those issues in life which nobody has been blessed to be sans with. You buckle, you fall, you say "Oh! To Hell with it, I can't take it anymore" and then again heave yourself up with a tenacity, never letting go of your vision. Time holds no meaning as you grapple with the numerous factors weighing by way of your other commitments, slots for all and still finding a slot to do with your passion, your calling.

Numerous wanted and unwanted advice from all quarters. It's left to your discretion to have the intelligence regarding what to pick and what to let go. The discouragement from 80% of the people not by being openly vocal but by a devious show of blatant indifference or personal remark at some point of time, casually dropped which makes you say "What the Hell man?" Fighting endlessly with yourself and still moving ahead with your head held high. Why this traumatic battle with you yourself and the others?

The answer is really so simple, by way of an allegory. You have suddenly seen a rainbow in the clouds and you hold the picture of that rainbow and start filling it with your colours. The colours spill but are merged again with those deft strokes, till the beauty of the rainbow shines forth in all it's component glory. Those who see the rainbow becoming a part of you, of someone who was merely a beautiful face till then, unable to accept this achievement, try with all their means to break the uniformity. It's here, where your passion for your passion steps forth, as you brace yourself to never let go of your passion, which has become your calling.

Proving therewith, your worth to yourself and once you have proven that, the battle has been won. The winning battle to be looked at by others with appreciation, always a welcome and if by squirming, matters not eventually, though it does impact at a certain point of time, when the butterflies were making their rounds in your tummy.

(My gut instinct favours me like my 'Guardian Angel'. I follow it to the T and have never found it wanting.)

184: ASPECT of LIFE***ACCEPTANCE

So much is taken for granted, not a thought flows in the direction of the hamper so full. Start counting your blessings and will you get lost in between. Still do we never stop cribbing, never stop comparing, never satiated with what we have. The wanting list reaches it's finished mark and lo and behold another list is on the threshold. The scramble once again begins and the vicious circle has a merry-go-round.

It's when we are deprived of these small pleasures of life which go unnoticed, that their real value hits us with a blow so hitting as to leave us rubbing our hands not with glee but with remorse. When it was within our reach to appreciate, we were too caught up with the next thing in offing and missed the mark.

So long a person is there everything about one such is again taken for granted. Leave alone appreciation, even acknowledging becomes too much of an effort. Yes criticism easily follows. Once the accepted presence is gone, all the virtues come striding to the fore. Overnight that person gets a halo round the head. Of what use now? That person left dejected and pained, craving for that iota of appreciation but none made their mark. Again we lose out on that simple aspect of humanity, of merely a word of praise but too much has been taken for granted, so much so that, that little bit of acceptance for the milestones crossed also becomes worth millions.

If life is a benediction of favours, life too reserves the right to deprive us of these favours, when it finds us unworthy of respecting them. It deprives us to bring unto us the realisation of how the smallest to the biggest unite to create that one happy whole and one missing link will bring about a collapse of the unified whole.

Render thanks for those little things in life which form the foundation of our lives, a life which asks for nothing but a respectful acceptance of the granted.

POEMS

1: TO BE IN SYNC

I'm in sync with the universe . . .
Coz my sub-conscious is in sync with the gifts that abound . . .
From the minutest to the biggest . . .
Catch the beat of my heart to the fullest . . .
It's so much beauty around . . .
The rustling, the blossoming, the buzzing, the twittering . . .
The twinkling, the gushing, the whisperings, the loving . . .
As though all merge into a comprehensive whole . . .
Making the heart sing and dance, a tapping so . . .
But can you get seeped into the vapours of the beauty around . . .
If you fail to feel the beauty of you, yourself deep down . . .
All will zero to nought . . .
So love yourself, as you are . . .
And be in sync with the gifts that abound.

2: BALANCE

The entire balance has got tilted . . .
And when the balance tips, holocaust tip-toes in . . .
The ravaging floods at one end . . .
And killing heat at the other . . .
Money being blown asunder . . .
The garbage food being partaken by the other . . .
Marriages on tenterhooks at the Altar . . .
What talk about the later . . .
Off-springs too busy with their partners . . .
The parents at the mercy of their neighbours . . .
Everything gone global . . .
Yet each one a loner . . .
Don't start the blame-game . . .
For will it go endless . . .
Do the little best you can from your end . . .
And endeavour to bring a smile at whichever end . . .
For the holocaust has stepped in with a vengeance . . .
Blowing everything asunder.

3: POTION

What is so delightful about this potion . . . ?
A colourful grapes decoction . . .
Makes the heart flutter and sing . . .
With wings high up in the cloudy rings . . .
A Knight in Armour with that charismatic swing . . .
Making a woman appear ten times prettier in the pink . . .
Morose spirits bounce back without a tinge . . .
All smiles scattered around with wings . . .
Shyness takes resort to the stage's wings . . .
And bellicose become some with a winning fling . . .
All dreams start washing the feet . . .
Life becomes a garden of hopes all fulfilled . . .
But this potion is not born with eternal life . . .
Soon the intoxicating vapours have their fill . . .
And the soaring high comes landing without a strip . . .
A bump and then a halt . . .
A heavy head with dreams all shattered amuck . . .
Oh! This grapes decoction . . .
What a capricious decoction?

(This is from a teetotaller, based on my observations.)

4: SWIIIIIIIIIIIIIIIIISH!

These are the times of 'use and throw' . . .
Swiiiiiiiiiiiiiiiiiiiish!
Everything goes out of the windows so . . .
Material things become redundant so . . .
After they have been used enough to be thrown so . . .
But my dear, relationships are also thrown to the winds so . . .
As though selective amnesia takes it's hold over the mind so . . .
All is forgotten in a jiffy so . . .
Simply coz the need is no longer so . . .
All that had to be stooged so . . .
Has done it's job to perfection so . . .
Why the Hell waste time and energy so . . .
Quickly dump it all out of the windows so . . .
The garbage van will come honking so . . .
And load it all, helter-skelter so . . .
Who cares now what was and what remains so . . .
'Use and throw' coz everyone is doing so.

5: FASHION

Fashion has you, fashion gets you . . .
Fashion buys you, fashion sells you . . .
It lurks in every corner of you . . .
Do it, wear it, flaunt it . . .
But dare overlook it . . .
Whether it suits you or grimaces at you . . .
Just ape it for it entices you . . .
Matters not if it brings you forth or dumps you down . . .
Matters not whether it's money well spent . . .
Or money flushed down the drains, indeed so very well spent . . .
Just do it coz it's fashion . . .
I say "Why not create your own style that becomes you?"
Coz if fashion makes a social statement . . .
Style makes a personal statement, never letting down you.

6: MARRIAGES

Marriages sure are made in Heaven . . .
For some it's jingle bells, jingle bells . . .
From the earth unto Heaven . . .
From the Altar till 'Death do us apart' . . .
From the merging of two identities into one . . .
Which death can't also do apart . . .
But for some are marriages made in Hell . . .
It's fire balls, fire balls revolving around . . .
Brick bats and thunder storms all around . . .
Had enough of the promises promised at the Altar . . .
Oh God, why the Hell wait for death to come sneaking after . . .
Quickly pick up the left pieces of you . . .
And run with hasty steps so true . . .
To the nearest divorce court, already so full . . .
Heave a sigh of relief and wonder . . .
"If marriages really are made in Heaven . . .
Then God-dammit why this Hell raging within the precincts of Heaven?"

7: LOVE IN THE POCKETS

Cupid the God of love . . .
May have been blind . . .
Half a century ago could have been the time . . .
Today love, if it's blind, can't be love . . .
The arrow before hitting . . .
Fathoms and weighs, Oh dickens . . .
The treasures stored and the favours in the digging . . .
The scales well measured and then the beckoning . . .
Each looking not into each other's eyes in the socket . . .
But holding each other with one hand in the other's pocket . . .
Oh dear, love is no longer sublime . . .
It's a well measured contract . . .
Which throws to the winds . . .
All that is blind.

8: NOT BORN A PRINCESS

She was not born a princess . . .
Exalted to the beauty and the magnificence of one she was . . .
A world of fairy-tales dreams came resting at her feet . . .
That dreamy sparkle in her eyes and the wishful smile . . .
As though swept her off her feet for a while . . .
But her buoyancy and naturalness could not let her be still . . .
And soon the strappings and the dos-and-don'ts of royalty . . .
Started strangulating her being . . .
Searched she did hither and thither . . .
For someone to love her for tether . . .
And when she did find a true lover . . .
Fate had it's own story to trigger . . .
And went to Heaven did Princess Diana with her lover Dodi . . .
But with that dreamy sparkle in her eyes and the wishful smile . . .
In the open arms of true love . . .
Did she freely breathe her last.

9: MOMENTS

Those moments blessed unto eternity . . .
Smiling that radiant smile of a dew-drop hanging from the ivy . . .
Spreading their charm like the ocean so vast . . .
Singing like the mermaid afloat a wave . . .
Benumbing my pores with their feel of delight . . .
Quenching my thirst with their moistened feel . . .
Widening my lips into a wistful smile . . .
As do I sit heaving a sigh . . .
Lost in those moments which are so much a part of my life . . .
The givers of those moments . . .
Many are gone, many are around . . .
Those who are gone, are still with their moments with me . . .
Those who are around will surely keep adding . . .
To those moments, with always their smiling, dewy feel . . . !

10: ME

To Hell with the fork, knife and spoon . . .
With all their tinkling cuckoos . . .
I love to gorge all my five fingers in my food . . .
To Hell with the brands and their smiles . . .
Too many tags to handle a pile . . .
I can wear a tuppence worth and create my own style . . .
To Hell with the so called social butterflies . . .
With all their plastic smiles and frivolous dimes . . .
I much rather be in the company of a person . . .
With knowledge and values though without a dime . . .
To Hell with the public image of mine . . .
Too much of an effort to adopt what is not mine . . .
I'd much rather be ME . . .
For who cares for what the others think of me . . . !

11: VAGABOND

Yes he was a vagabond . . .
People sneered at him so . . .
Because he had no home to call his own . . .
Because all the clothes he had were what he wore . . .
Because not even a meal was promised to him since yore . . .
Yet to me was he a vagabond?
No! To me was he an awakening so fond . . .
A treasure house of knowledge was he . . .
An emancipated soul so free . . .
A peace so calm and full of glee . . .
A day spent with him so fulfilling to the lees . . .
Because every second did he live . . .
Sans any baggage was he . . .
To me he was not a vagabond . . .
A person well versed with the innuendoes of life was he . . . !

12: NIGHTINGALE

The nightingale on the floral branch sang in mirth . . .
The husky rustling of the leaves as though it's melody . . .
The gushing water of the brook beneath . . .
Gurgling and lending happiness to the welcome notes . . .
Nature holding hands to a rollicking song . . .
At a distance did I stand . . .
A lone observer . . .
Imbibing every bit of the nightingale's song . . .
The warmth of nature's togetherness . . .
A spontaneous giving . . .
Unconditional . . .
At a distance did I stand . . .
A lone observer . . .
A specimen of mankind . . . !

13: HOLDING HANDS

To be able to hold hands . . .
Across oceans . . .
To be able to hold hands . . .
Whatever be the caste, colour or creed . . .
To be able to hold hands . . .
Over years which define age . . .
To be able to hold hands . . .
Despite the adornments or the rags . . .
To be able to hold hands . . .
Beyond the barriers of relationships . . .
To be able to hold hands . . .
Simply because you are you and I am I . . .
Is what gets clasped betwixt the hands . . .
To stay for eternity . . .
When the last breath also is unable to separate . . .
This love so sublime and true . . . !

14: AMEN

When the heart is gone . . .
The will is gone . . .
The spirit is gone . . .
A resounding hollowness around . . .
Engulfs you . . .
Whispers and shadows hovering around . . .
Ask you . . .
"Why these gamut of emotions, do we see flitting so?" . . .
Say you "What emotions . . . ?
Emotions did I leave behind in the whispers and the shadows . . .
Thus it is what you so espy . . .
My heart I gave to Him . . .
Nothing now remains . . .
But this wholesome silence . . .
And my spirit and will one with His . . .
Nothing, and still everything remains so . . . !"

15: ONENESS

Love is rising above the level of consciousness . . .
When I and nature become one . . .
When the personalised goes into the abstract . . .
An all expansive sensation of oneness . . .
The soul as though frolicking with the fragrance around . . .
The mind at rest amidst the ethereal hues . . .
Joys and sorrows lose their sense of belonging . . .
This 'I' gets subterfuged into infinity . . .
It's then that love smiles forth in its real essence . . .
Beyond the bondage of human existence . . . !

16: BEAUTY

Anything beautiful catches the eyes and the sighs . . .
It differentiates not betwixt the rich and the poor . . .
All are equally welcome to its open door . . .
Its heart so big, for all to reside . . .
It's when this beauty becomes the treasure for those . . .
Personalised it becomes so . . .
'You' and 'Me' starts to knock at the door . . .
No longer an open door . . .
The rich and the poor start making the difference . . .
Beauty starts to get robbed of its essence . . .
Oh! Ye fools, little do you realise . . .
This beauty is only skin-deep . . .
Today it's here, tomorrow it's not there . . .
Still do you breathe, 'You' and 'Me' . . . !

17: OH!

She wined and she dined . . .
Making the world a merry-go-round . . .
Her sensuality missed by none . . .
Those red pouting scarlet lips a lover's delight . . .
The come hither looks from those drunken eyes . . .
Made many a hearts swoon at their sight . . .
Tried to lose herself did she . . .
In the arms of all who came her way . . .
Yet none stayed long enough to wipe her tears . . .
Those sobs did she let out on her pillow at night . . .
Lonely at heart was she so . . .
Till one night the abandonment stalked her breaths . . .
And ended her life she did . . .
Downing a bottle of sleeping pills . . .
"No amount of money can buy you happiness" . . .
This secret of life, she Marilyn Monroe had understood.

18: MOODINESS

They say I'm a moody person . . .
Given to the high and low tides am I . . .
A laughter now and a tear there . . .
Tensed and a descending calm now . . .
Angry like the whipping up of the waves . . .
And soon a descending peace . . .
An arrogance tough to counter . . .
Yet, sit do I with a tramp . . .
Enjoying a tete-e-tete so drawn . . .
Childish fancies and a wise lady's wisdom . . .
Do a somersaulting act so dear . . .
Yes! I do stand to be as moody as can be . . .
Being bridled and harnessed I can't be . . .
Suffocated to death will I be . . .
For hiding myself beneath layers of 'not me' . . .
Oh! At least have I got wings . . .
What if they are moody wings?

19: AS I AM

Wow! It always feel so cuddly and feathery to be just me . . .
Naked, devoid of all that superficial baggage . . .
Making their hearts and minds ever so heavy with all that baggage . . .
Their minds scampering faster than their heart-beats . . .
To wrestle with the thoughts of the person in front and overpower his heart-beats . . .
What to say, what not to say . . .
How to stand and smile that sick smile, to say just the right thing to say . . .
All for that stupid yearning to be everyone's darling . . .
Endeavouring to wear multi-layered clothing to be that darling . . .
Hiding and hiding that real self . . .
No matter what the effort and the sleepless nights which get lost in hiding that real self . . .
Oh Dickens! Lemme be 'ME' . . .
As I am and as I do stand in the nude . . .
Love me or hate me . . .
Find me or avoid me . . .
Who cares a damn . . .
For I am not scared to be what I truly am . . .
Behind closed doors or in front of open doors . . .
Hence no baggage ever . . .
So do I sleep as peacefully as a babe in the crib and will so forever.

20: PETTICOAT GOVERNMENT

Ah! This petticoat government . . .
Who killed the cat the first night is the winning vote for this government . . .
And if it happens to be the wife, well then it becomes a petticoat government . . .
No fixed tenure for this government . . .
An everlasting tenure is the bliss of this government . . .
No constitutional laws to be followed by this government . . .
Laws made and broken at will are the pillars of this government . . .
Emergency imposed as and when are the controlling factors of this government . . .
No democracy or republicanism, dare step near this government . . .
A dictatorship which puts to shame Hitler's government . . .
The poor and the only subject—the husband . . .
Has no courts to spill his woes against this government . . .
He 'heave-hoes' his precious life under the tyranny of this government . . .
And at night cries out to his dear father . . .
"Oh! Why didn't you teach me how to kill the cat the first night . . .
The way you killed the cat the first night . . . ?"
And I grew up dreaming hollering, shouting and throwing my weight around . . .
Not hiding under the petticoat of this petticoat government.

21: CHARITY

"Do not let your left hand know what your right hand is doing . . ."
Nowadays, let the world know what you are doing . . .
Do charity but in full public glare . . .
In the media and the paparazzi's glare . . .
With that howler of a smile stretched on the face . . .
Putting indeed to shame the smile on Mona Lisa's face . . .
Seeing and hearing endless about 'your' beneficial deed . . .
Doling out a million and making a crore from that deed . . .
A 'Messiah' indeed, for those in need . . .
Basking and snoring under the blanket of their need . . .
Little do these 'public image' crazy people realise . . .
The real value of their giving is lost . . .
The moment their hired trumpets blast . . .
Their charity around, for then everything does blast . . .
Real charity is when . . .
The receiver is blissfully unaware of the giver . . .
For then can he don the mantle of the 'Messiah' . . .
The true giver.

22: COMPULSIVE TALKERS

. . . and then there are those indeed, the compulsive talkers . . .
Who go on and on and on, their bellies full like gossip mongers . . .
As though the world is going to end the next minute . . .
So keep blabbing as much as you can, for you never know what'll happen so the next minute . . .
The conversation never begins because the monologue never ends . . .
If by chance you do manage to butt in, as quickly are you cut short before you can end . . .
Time gets wrapped betwixt the circle of great grandpa's and the latest arrival en route . . .
My mind sure gets lost in the rigmarole of such hues . . .
In abject daze do I sit, wishing fervently for this non-stop buzzing to fuse . . .
Hours have been whiled away with my head heavy but not with booze . . .
Oh dear! Have a heart, not everyone is blessed like you . . .
To go on and on and on . . .
For you never know when the world will come to an end, heads on.

23: BEAUTY AND BRAINS

Beauty and brains don't go together . . .
Is this a fallacy or cockiness clubbed together . . . ?
"Oh! She's a blonde, her brains the size of a peanut . . ."
Or those who blab so, their brains are the size of a peanut . . .
But then again beauty is a term which none can book . . .
Beauty sure lies in the beholder's looks to book . . .
It has no numerical quotients nor yardsticks to hook . . .
The statistics are as fluid as the looks that hook . . .
Tis a fact, the beautiful need not worry so about their looks . . .
And so with their self esteem ride high on their looks . . .
But beware of this near fatal combination of beauty and brains, so true . . .
For men sure become less intelligent in the face of beauty and brains, so true . . .
A startling potion which make men bow in reverence so blind . . .
Before this legendary unison of the apples of beauty and brains, so fine.

24: SHE

Bedraggled and weary she sat by the roadside . . .
Time nor tide, neither seemed to be on her side . . .
Yet a dignity shone forth from her eyes . . .
A character from her bearing which captivated my eyes . . .
Both complemented her bent figure by the roadside . . .
My steps faltered and halted by her on her side . . .
A toothless smile flickered on her lips . . .
As welcoming tears glistened in her misty eyes dropping to her lips . . .
I softly wiped the fallen pearls . . .
And felt a caring warmth on my hands with the pearls . . .
Such an intense feel of love and joy did I feel when she gripped my hands . . .
As the magnificence of a villa or sipping tea from a Venetian cup can never give . . .
I crushed her wizened figure in a bear hug as a bear hug can be . . .
And complimented her saying "It's been over a year since I lost my mother so . . .
But today I felt the same magnitude of love and happiness . . .
As I had always felt within the circle of her loving arms."

25: SMALL JOYS

The fish' thought the whole ocean was theirs . . .
Till they did found themselves on the sandy shore . . .
And realised what a succour the ocean was of theirs . . .
The birds thought the whole world was theirs . . .
Till they find themselves caged . . .
And realised the beauty of the sky and the trees was not always theirs . . .
She was in the Seventh Heaven with her arms full . . .
Till one by one a lot was taken away . . .
And she happened to realise those were never to return, making her arms full . . .
None fathom or thank for those small joys which abound . . .
Making life an event so blissful and true . . .
Tis when you are deprived of those tiny atoms of freedom which abound . . .
Do you realise the significance of those blessings so true.

26: "YES BOSS"

"Yes boss . . . yes boss . . . yes boss . . ."
The boss's ears are attuned to this "yes boss" . . .
Struts in like a strutting peacock . . .
But makes other's dance to his tune like a peacock . . .
Uses an escalator to be where he wished to be, the boss . . .
Making the underneaths swing to his whims as, the boss . . .
In a galaxy of sycophants beams he . . .
An ace hum-bug though he may be . . .
What will his employees not do to please . . .
Coz their jobs will be at stake if they don't sing his tune to please . . .
I thank the Lord for either being without the calibre or the ambition . . .
To keep "yessing" the boss in right or wrong because of my ambition . . .
Thank Lord, sleeping and waking I don't have to have nightmares of "yes boss" . . .
I'd much rather dream bountiful dreams of beautiful dreams . . .
As they are meant to be, please of no "yes boss".

(There are of course bosses who well nigh do justice to their position but it's an ebbing syndrome.)

27: PASSION

What is life sans any passion . . . ?
Almost akin to breathing hollow breaths, when there is no passion . . .
Living your life with an ardour and ecstasy, in pursuit of that passion . . .
Unleashing it to flow relentlessly, which is passion . . .
Try to girdle it and will you make a laughing stock of your passion . . .
A direction which gives those beatific linings to your life and it's passion . . .
A mind and heart which gets madly lost to the intoxication of the passion . . .
Oblivious to the surroundings when trapped in the fumes of that passion . . .
Oh! What would I do if I had not this writing passion . . .
I do so lose myself in my thoughts and emotions . . .
As do they flow cuddling my years with all their smiles and tears, in my passion . . .
Making me live and not simply exist, gripping the hands of my passion.

28: BUNCH OF CRIMSON JOY

The car stopped at the crossing before the red light . . .
A small girl's pretty face pressed against the window screen . . .
A stalk of red rose waving in her hand against the screen . . .
The chirpy happiness radiated her angelic face . . .
Her eyes and lips smiled a smile lighting her beatific face . . .
Mesmerised I did bring down the window screen . . .
To hear a giggle from a bunch of crimson roses which waved in the open sans the screen . . .
Just a screen betwixt the boundless joy and my furrowed eye-brows . . .
With everything in my lap but why still this baggage on my brows . . .
I stretched my arm for the bunch of crimson joy . . .
Handing across more than the price of the ardent joy . . .
The face so shone with a light so blessed . . .
A happiness which glowed from happiness itself . . .
Oh! Sighed I "What will I not give to share this happiness so wild . . ."
As did I caress my cheeks making them crimson so wild . . .
Giving a tweak on those chubby cheeks . . .
Just a window screen betwixt the happiness and the furrowed brows.

29: SOMERSAULT

There was a time when it was the prerogative of a clown to somersault . . .
Today time does a much better somersault . . .
What was is no more . . .
And what is, better not be . . .
The tide of time comes raging with a speeding somersault . . .
Throwing hither and thither what it took generations to lay the foundations
for . . .
Because the easiest thing for the advent of something new . . .
Is to throw out what was there in lieu . . .
And so are we helpless witnesses to the somersaulting dances around . . .
Name any sphere and will you never draw a blank or a fuse . . .
The "tap-e-tap" of the changes ensue . . .
Dis-balancing the balance with a rollicking force that "shoos" . . .
Making us clowns in our own eyes which "boos" . . .
Still are we slaves to this somersaulting dance with it's colourful hues . . . ?

30: HONOUR

If there is anything more juxtaposed . . .
It's our dear 'men' being called 'dogs' . . .
They should indeed feel honoured to be called so . . .
Though they have none of the qualities of a 'dog' . . .
A dog is loyal, how many men can boast of not having a roving eye and thus being loyal . . .
A dog is non-judgemental, men drive their wives crazy by being ever so judgemental . . .
A dog is un-demanding, men drive their wives up the wall with their non-ending demands . . .
A dog is patient, men pull the roof down if any of their things get misplaced for a lark . . .
Oh yes! There is certainly one thing where 'men' and 'dogs' are not juxtaposed . . .
If dogs run after bitches, then do men never spare a 'birdie in hand' for the Dickens . . .
So let the 'men' feel honoured by being called 'dogs' . . .
An honour is an honour after all.

31: GOSSIP MONGERING

Rip, rip, rip, apart . . .
A person's reputation ever so fast . . .
Seasoning with salt and pepper wherever you can . . .
Making the person the centre of the evening's yarns . . .
With what mirth amidst the clinking of glasses . . .
Does the 'nothing to do better' company guffaws and refills those pegs in the glasses . . .
The person who happens to be the sacrificial goat of the evening . . .
Is innocently unaware of his shameless de-clothing . . .
But never forget this one simple truth of this gossip mongering . . .
The moment your back will be turned to the guffaws and the clinking . . .
You will also be the butt of this shameless stripping . . .
So my dear!!! Think of how it will be so hurting . . .
When you see your undies or lingerie hanging at a crossing?

32: SHADOWS AND WHISPERS

See how the petals of a flower are blown away . . .
See how the leaves of a tree are blown away . . .
Each in it's direction, wherever the breeze takes them away . . .
So also is every moment with it's smiles and tears ticked away . . .
Into the misty haze do the shadows and the whispers hide away . . .
If remembered, those beautiful times can never be snatched away . . .
If whisked away by the breeze, then every moment is washed away . . .
The rationale will say "but so is the way of the world, memories are memories after all" they'll say . . .
And an emotional fool like me will say "but it's memories which give succour to your life" I'll say . . .
Try wiping them out but never will they get erased . . .
That's the beauty of those memories . . .
Aren't they always by your side to stay?

33: REAL FROM THE UNREAL

Oh! Dickens, tis indeed tough . . .
To fathom the real from the un-real . . .
The colour of the hair . . .
From burgundy, to chestnut, to bleached, hair . . .
Those fluttering eyelashes . . .
Glued to the heavy eyelids with the false eyelashes . . .
The tantalising blue, grey or hazel contacts . . .
Slipped on carefully onto the real colour, minus the contacts . . .
The cosmetic attachments well hidden underneath the clothing . . .
Giving the cool, mouth gaping, right contours and the curves above the clothing . . .
Oh! Dickens, tis indeed tough . . .
When the real character lies craftily hidden . . .
Under the real character, not so becoming . . .
What talk of fake appearances . . .
Which can be bought off the shelf, though never for a pittance . . .
When the actual character . . .
Belies all and sundry worth a pittance.

VANDANA SINHA

34: ALONE

She stood alone in the meadow . . .
Looking at the vistas beyond . . .
A lone figure yet so resplendent in the loneliness . . .
As her past brought those childish dreams back into her eyes and smile . . .
As her past educated her with the nuances of life . . .
As her past gave a direction to her life so right . . .
As did her present engulf her with it's presence so bright . . .
As did her present give her no cause for regret so trite . . .
As did her present be like a babe of the past and the future combined . . .
As did the future beckon her with it's winsome smile . . .
As did her future make her look beyond the horizon so fine . . .
As did her future hold out it's arms to cuddle her with all it's might . . .
Yes, she stood alone in the meadow . . .
But never is she alone . . .
For her past, present and the future . . .
Are her Guardian Angels which never make her feel alone.

35: CHANGE

Change is the only static thing in life . . .
But the basic ingredients of the character do remain the same . . .
As do they rear their heads in those moments of crisis . . .
A person struts around at a party . . .
A gallery of flamboyance is he . . .
Walks by a waiter holding a tray of delights . . .
'Bang' he bumps into the charismatic style . . .
A volley of the choicest abuses do make a merry-go-round . . .
As does all his flamboyance drops 'plop' to the ground . . .
Another equally well turned out in the same scenario . . .
Will hold the waiter by the shoulder and ask with all concern . . .
"Hope you didn't get hurt my dear?" . . .
The tuxedo of both got equally ruined, my dear . . .
But the former showed up his class, if class it was, my dear . . .
And the latter's class never got shaken by the bump, my dear . . .
So the real character of one . . .
Does show up with a bump, my dear.

36: COFFIN

What is so alluring about the coffin . . . ?
Time, money and distance is all shoved aside to be by the coffin . . .
To pray for the departed soul, to rest in peace, which is no longer breathing . . .
To pay respect to the mere mortal remains which has been deprived of all feelings . . .
What is the use of wiping those tears in the perfumed hanky . . .
When time, money and distance was but more important . . .
Than being by the side of the person, no more, with love and compassion . . .
Bringing those smiling eyes to light with adoration . . .
Fulfilling a life's dream in those precious moments with fascination . . .
But then everything took precedence over those emotions . . .
What is the use now of writhing your body with tears of affliction . . .
Your tears will dry betwixt the layers of your handkerchief . . .
As you do cry by the side of the coffin . . .
The life, the soul has flown into the unknown, into infinity . . .
For it is the coffin which has pulled you to it's side . . .
What indeed is so alluring about this coffin?

37: CELEBRITY

Ah!!! . . .
A celebrity . . .
Works through life to don the mantle of one . . .
And then dons dark glasses to avoid being recognized as one . . .
A celebrity one can become out of merit . . .
Or nuisance value which rejects all merit . . .
All efforts pushed towards being one such . . .
Ranging from the positive to the negative on such . . .
A talent projected surpassing all the other's talents . . .
Scaling the clouds with the raving interviews of the talents . . .
Or hiring barking dogs to create a nuisance value . . .
And scaling the clouds on the barking of the nuisance value . . .
Juxtaposed . . .
Ah!!!
A celebrity . . .
Whether worth the talent . . .
Or the hired barking dogs yapping of the nuisance . . .
A celebrity, is a celebrity . . .
The cake for the news and the media to munch upon . . .
With the added salt and pepper to hype upon.

38: CHIEF GUEST

Oh! The poor chief guest or the beloved chief guest . . .
The clamouring as does he step out of the car . . .
Dozens of garlands do hang like a noose . . .
As do people topple over each other . . .
To laden his neck with the noose . . .
Like a robot does he walk hither and thither . . .
Not knowing which way to go, all in a tether . . .
Each falling over the other to stooge as any favours . . .
While the chief guest is there for a lager . . .
Sandwiched betwixt the fawning people for a picture . . .
As do step on his toes to get a little closer . . .
As though it matters to him who the Tom, Dick or Harry is standing closer . . .
I always watch from a distance, the entire scenario . . .
And marvel at the plight of the poor chief guest . . .
As does he stand trying to catch hold of his bearings . . .
The so called beloved chief guest.

39: CHAIR

Is it the chair which gets the person . . . ?
Or is it the person which gets the chair . . .
Perhaps it's both because only a dumb head gets influenced so . . .
The poor chair cries as it squirms . . .
Under the weight of an idiot who has plonked himself . . .
And leaves not a stone unturned to fan himself . . .
The learned and the wise pay obeisance . . .
Cursing the occupant under their breath with all their might . . .
As do they stand with bended knees . . .
To keep a hold over their own chair . . .
The person also gets the chair . . .
With the head turned at degrees 90 . . .
Does such a one gets bloated enough . . .
The weight spilling much beyond the chair . . .
A demi-God if not a God is he in his own eyes . . .
A man of signatures is he in the chair . . .
Brains don't matter as long as the chair is there . . .
Little do these bloated heads realise . . .
How short lived is the life of the chair . . .
Once it bids adieu all will be gone . . .
In a matter of seconds from the sky to the earth . . .
Will he come hurtling down . . .
So grace your chair with dignity and respect . . .
So that the chair cries when your name-plate comes down.

40: MUMMY

A lady who held you spell-bound with her beauty so Indian . . .
As artistes dream to be treasured betwixt the strokes of the brush . . .
How crestfallen was he at her refusal to be captured as much . . .
An elegant grace and a suffused dignity . . .
Which did make her stand apart in a milling crowd . . .
Her charm hid so much in her demeanour and simplicity . . .
The pulsating warmth and love ever shone from every bit of her being . . .
A wisdom which put to rest many a doubts . . .
Like a pearl in an oyster shell . . .
Was she protected and doted upon by her husband so dear . . .
Yet did she face the insurmountable loss with a bravery sans any fear . . .
Living the years with a dignified independence as became only her . . .
Always giving never ever expecting . . .
A lady with a presence and substance unmatched . . .
A Mummy whose daughter am I so proud to be . . .
A Mummy who is forever and forever and will ever be.

41: PAPA

He was a man of few words . . .
Not another till now . . .
A presence which brought a regard of sorts . . .
Hardly ever did he speak beyond his thoughts . . .
A gravity which could never be looked past . . .
A wisdom and far-sightedness were his trade-marks
A heart brimming with so much love and care . . .
Yet a disciplinarian was he . . .
A stick which he wielded but never for free . . .
A connoisseur of antiques was he . . .
Gathering a collection of rarities . . .
The wondrous beauty of which did make the eyes freeze . . .
Of course I was his pampered lot . . .
A spoilt brat as ever could be . . .
My anchor in life was he . . .
Left me ever so suddenly that completely shattered me . . .
Yet his he always by my side . . .
As I do move on in life . . .
A prodigy of his wisdom and love always by my side . . .
Like my Papa none other can be.

42: MEN

Oh! Dear . . .
These men surely find a place in my heart . . .
Even though they may not make a place in a historian's heart . . .
Toiling from morn till night . . .
With their wives making a hole in their pocket sides . . .
Without a twinge of remorse do they go berserk from all sides . . .
A li'l in the parlour . . .
A li'l in the stores . . .
A li'l at poker . . .
And a li'l, a li'l, wherever they can . . .
The golden goose is there to provide for it all . . .
For either his love goes too strong . . .
Or hen-pecked is he to be just as strong . . .
Or coz it becomes a man's privilege . . .
And I say 95% of his image . . .
Is made or marred by the woman clinging on to his arm . . .
So do they rub their ass off . . .
For reasons which go beyond, where all logic gets lost . . .
Oh! Dear . . .
My heart goes out for such a lot . . .
Lemme pay a tribute to their lot . . .
Dole out with both your hands . . .
For it takes just a drop of the hat . . .
For such painted dolls . . .
To be in the arms of someone, maybe just by your side door . . . !

43: OPEN DOOR

The moon does smilingly give it's way to the sun . . .
As every night sees a morning . . .
The rustling autumn leaves on the earth . . .
Leave their abode for the sprouting of leaves so new . . .
The storm with it's thunder and rain . . .
Clears up with a rainbow for a break . . .
That catch in the throat with the spilling of tears . . .
Umpteen times do follow with a catchy grin . . .
Standing alone with the doors all shut . . .
To suddenly witness an open door . . .
That ultimate breath which breaks so many hearts . . .
Opens the way to the freedom of the spirit so large . . .
So does life have it's hiccups . . .
To be braced and countered . . .
Remembering always . . .
Every night sees a morning . . . !

44: ENIGMA

To be as elusive as an enigma . . .
Shrouded in mystery and mysticism . . .
As transient as a mirage . . .
So attractive to the eyes yet slips the feel . . .
The husky, wanting, ringing laughter . . .
So close, yet belies the sound so near . . .
Impish eyes, lost in their own . . .
Well within reach, yet so beyond . . .
A voice indeed welcoming and warm . . .
Suddenly sounds indifferent and drawn . . .
Humble and modest to a point . . .
Yet an arrogance which goes beyond a point . . .
Loved and adored as much . . .
Questioned no less, if not as much . . .
Everyone's darling she can't be . . .
As elusive as an enigma she continues to be . . .
Hidden in a small corner of this earth, is she . . .
Making her presence felt, when she wants it to be.

45: NRI

So in walked an N.R.I . . .
Brandishing all his brands like a 'mannequin of brandism' . . .
"Hi guys" he smiled and I said "How do you do" . . .
"I'm fine" he replied and I smiled and thought . . .
(You have gone one down in the rung of the ladder, my dear) . . .
And then started a tornado against everything Indian . . .
(You have gone down a second rung of the ladder, my dear) . . .
Unable to hold myself so, did I butt in . . .
"Where were you born and brought up, my dear?" . . .
"In this country, which you call India" . . .
"Oh!" said I "So it seems you were re-born again in another country, my dear?"
He smirked and said "Yes, what a relief to be re-born so again" . . .
(You have slipped down the entire length of the ladder, my dear) . . .
With my patience, all gone to the winds did I say . . .
"Oh! Yes what a relief for India too, to have done away with the likes of you."

46: SELFISH MODE

Verily! All relationships revolve around that selfish mode . . .
The wedding vows are thrown to the winds, once the foot-steps leave the threshold of the Church . . .
And the relationship soon dwindles to "You scratch my back and I'll scratch yours" . . .
Love these days has become a commodity shamelessly called love . . .
As do lovers weigh all the pros and cons, which belies the purity of something so sublime as love . . .
Seldom are friendships on an honouring ground . . .
They soon hang on that flimsy give and take rope which goes below the ground . . .
All the tags to the in-law category do so leave one dumbfounded . . .
Rest as they do on a platform repugnant with expectations, envy and competition, never so to be founded . . .
The children seldom are able to fulfil their mantle of duties . . .
So engrossed are they in their own lives with their duties . . .
The only relationship which crosses the boundary of this selfish mode . . .
Is that of the mother's unyielding love for her children so dear . . .
Every breath of hers, no matter how heavy be the breath, is ever so dear . . .
Verily! All other relationships can never be so dear.

(There are exceptions of course but they are as rare as the four leaf clover.)

47: THE FAIRY WORLD

Oh! To be once again enmeshed in that fairy-world of fairy tales . . .
To get lost in that dreamy, tender feel of those fairy-tales . . .
The midnight gong chimes the magical twelve . . .
And Cinderella goes running leaving her pretty shoe as the clock chimes twelve . . .
The enchanting long tresses go down from the window . . .
As does Rapunzel's Prince Charming climbs up the tresses to the window . . .
The goblins and the elves with their twinkling eyes and cheeky smiles . . .
Pamper little Snow-white till she giggles and smiles . . .
The little feet so slip, as to bring her rattling down into a new world . . .
As Alice in the Wonderland frolics with her Dinah, Tweedledee and Tweedledum of the fairy world . . .
Oh! My childish meanderings, what nostalgia is this . . .
If only I could open the doors of this fairy-world, once again, for utter bliss?